Fighting with
the Commandos

Fighting with the Commandos

The Recollections of Stan Scott
No. 3 Commando

Edited by
NEIL BARBER

Pen & Sword
MILITARY

First published in Great Britain in 2008 by
PEN & SWORD MILITARY
an imprint of
Pen & Sword Books Ltd
47 Church Street, Barnsley, South Yorkshire, S70 2AS

Copyright © Stan Scott and Neil Barber, 2008

ISBN 978-1-84415-732-7

Typeset by Concept, Huddersfield, West Yorkshire
Printed and bound in England by CPI UK

Pen & Sword Books Ltd incorporates the Imprints of
Pen & Sword Aviation, Pen & Sword Maritime, Pen & Sword Military,
Wharncliffe Local History, Pen & Sword Select,
Pen & Sword Military Classics and Leo Cooper

For a complete list of Pen & Sword titles please contact
PEN & SWORD BOOKS LIMITED
47 Church Street, Barnsley, South Yorkshire, S70 2AS, England
E-mail: enquiries@pen-and-sword.co.uk
Website: www.pen-and-sword.co.uk

To the 70th Young Soldier Battalions
and those who went on to wear the red and the green lids.

Contents

List of Maps

List of Abbreviations

ACF	Army Cadet Force
ADS	Advanced Dressing Station
AWOL	Absent without leave
CMF	Central Mediterranean Forces
CO	Commanding Officer
DP	Displaced Person
DSO	Distinguished Service Order
DZ	Dropping Zone
ETA	Estimated Time of Arrival
ETD	Estimated Time of Departure
HE	High Explosive
HP	Hire Purchase
LMG	Light Machine Gun
LST	Landing Ship, Tank
LZ	Landing Zone
MC	Military Cross
MEF	Middle East Forces
MG	Machine Gun
MM	Military Medal
MT	Motor Transport
NAAFI	Navy, Army and Air Force Institutes
NCO	Non Commissioned Officer
OC	Officer Commanding
OP	Observation Point
POW	Prisoner Of War
PTI	Physical Training Instructor
RASC	Royal Army Service Corps

RE	Royal Engineer
RTO	Railway Transport Officer
RTU	Returned to Unit
STAG	Standing Tall At Gate
TSM	Troop Sergeant Major
VC	Victoria Cross

Currency Equivalents:

Halfpenny = no decimal equivalent
Penny = ½p
Sixpence = 2½p
A Shilling (known as a bob) = 5p
Two Bob = 10p
Half a crown = 12½p
Ten Bob = 50p

Preface

The aura earned by the Commandos in the Second World War endures to this day. This is quite an achievement when you consider that the Army Commando units were disbanded immediately the conflict came to an end. However, during this short existence their fighting reputation and place in history was sealed. Official histories explain in general terms the raids and involvement in the campaigns in Europe and the Far East, but what were these men like? What did it take to become a Commando? Well, these recollections by Stan Scott provide some idea of the qualities and attitude that were necessary. Many volunteered from Young Soldier Battalions, which had been set up to accommodate those old enough to enlist but who were too young to serve overseas. They saw themselves as 'Churchill's Boys', and had followed the debacle in France and witnessed the Blitz on British cities. They wanted to get back at the enemy at the first possible opportunity.

Our paths first crossed about ten years ago, outside the Mairie in Amfreville, a few miles north-east of Pegasus Bridge. We discussed the liberation of the village, in which he had taken part, and having interviewed many veterans over the previous few years, his memory immediately stood out as being among the sharpest I had heard. I subsequently found that the reasons for this were his extremely inquisitive, active mind, and that after leaving the Army he had continued to live like a soldier as a civilian, the same discipline, the same attitude, retaining his interest in all things to do with the British Army. In the years since that day in Normandy, I have lost count of the interviews that have taken place and the correspondence supplied, but through all of this I never ceased to be amazed at his knowledge of the Army and particularly of soldier-ing. As I gradually got to know him, he recounted matters of his childhood and the journey that ultimately led to him join Peter Young's famous No. 3 Commando. However, it wasn't the usual kind of information, but a view of life during the war, from civilian aspects to soldiering in the Commandos, always detailed and without any holds barred. His first real action was on D-Day, and so this, plus the following few months of static warfare in Normandy form quite a large section of this account. In places it is brutal, in others poignant, but as can sometimes be found in such scenarios, humour is never far away. It provides a clear picture of the reality of life at that time and of day-to-day warfare.

There are several things that have annoyed Stan over the years with regard to 'generally accepted facts', which are constantly copied from book to book. One of them is the belief, generated by the film of *The Longest Day*, that Lord Lovat was the first Commando to arrive at Pegasus Bridge on D-Day. It is well known within the Commandos that this is simply not true and can be testified to by members of Stan's 3 Troop, 3 Commando and also Troops of 6 Com-mando. Other similar matters may be self-evident and will certainly generate debate, which he will be only too happy about!

Following the disbandment of the Army Commandos there is a fascinating chapter on his life as a military policeman in Brussels tackling black marketeers, and also in Germany on war crimes duty.

In 1947, unable to get into the Parachute Regiment due to Army bureaucracy, he became a 'civvy'.

Twenty-three years later he joined the Territorial Army Volunteer Reserve, and began training cadets (including officers), encouraging other youths to join in his own characteristic manner. He retired from this at eighty years of age! Stan remains an active, imposing figure with a passion for the Commandos, and since the demise of the Commando Association, is now the Chairman of the newly-formed Commando Veterans Association (CVA). They have nurtured close links with such units as the Royal Marine Com-mandos, 29 Commando RA and 59 Commando RE, who continue to maintain their memory and high reputation.

It is very pleasing that the larger part of his experience is now in print, as he has given so much to the British Army both during and after the war.

I am also proud that he has allowed me to put this together, and would like to think that I now qualify as a friend, although I would not have the nerve to presume such a thing. I will have to ask!

Although particularly famed for their raids, the Commandos' actions in an infantry role during the Normandy campaign and later through North-West Europe, have largely been overlooked. Hopefully, Stan's account will help to redress this imbalance a little.

Neil Barber
August 2007

Editor's Acknowledgements

With this being a biography, there are not too many people to thank! However, I would like to relay my gratitude to Dave Wellesley and Michael Pine-Coffin for advice and the editing of drafts at various stages; to Lieutenant Colonel Stanford for writing the introduction, Councillor John Mander and Terry McCann for their accounts of life with Stan in the Army Cadet Force, and to Stan Scott Junior for putting me in contact with them. Scotty knows nothing of their input, so it should be a nice surprise. I would also like to thank Stan's wife, Pam, for her hospitality during my frequent visits to their home. Thanks also to Brigadier Henry Wilson at Pen & Sword and George Chamier, the copy editor. Finally, thanks to my ever patient wife, Caroline.

Neil Barber

Introduction

When I was asked to write an introduction for Stan Scott my first thoughts were what an honour; and secondly where do I start; and how, in a few paragraphs, do you encapsulate such a character? I then spent the next few hours with a military colleague trying to find biographies to get some ideas. We then sat in our vehicle and just chatted about the times and experiences I have shared with Stan. I decided this was probably the best way forward. No flowery prose, just straight and direct. Just like Stan.

I first met Stan at 16 Company, The Royal Green Jackets, Army Cadet Force in 1980. I had just decided, through a newspaper advert, to become an ACF Instructor. Strange really, as I had no military experience whatsoever. I walked into his office, he eyed me up and down, and read the letter of introduction. He then lifted a Bren machine gun. 'Is this a heavy machine gun or light?' I looked at it and thought, 'Looks pretty heavy to me.' 'Heavy', I said with confidence. Wrong! Stan just exhaled loudly and started that night with my initial military training.

Some people are lucky to experience a person, who outside of their immediate family has a moulding impact on their early life. I have been extremely fortunate to meet two such individuals. Stan was one of those.

My time with Stan was centred on the cadets. Since then, with the foundation of Stan and others, I, like many other people who have been trained by him, have enjoyed a successful career in the Territorial Army and on Operational Tours worldwide for over twenty-six years. All this can be traced back to that first meeting and the dedication of this man.

I cannot imagine how many cadets have passed through Stan's hands. To some he was a father figure they lacked at home, to others the figure of discipline so much required now as it was then, to others someone to talk to and receive advice from. It is interesting to note that some cadets are now senior officers and warrant officers in the cadet force and TA, I am no doubt sure due to this man's advice and direction.

Stan is a forthright man who up until very recently was still very much active in the ACF. On exercises in the 1990s he was still to be found out in the field offering words of wisdom and sleeping under plastic sheets, this when most people would be at home with pipe and slippers. He exhibited an encyclopaedic knowledge of fieldcraft and a willingness to get involved at any level, so long as it was for the benefit of the cadets. Stan never sought praise for praise's sake, his focus and main effort was always the cadets.

He had a career that stretched all the way back to the Second World War and what a fascinating career that was. An insight you will no doubt get in this book. He always wore his Green Beret from the Army Commandos, he just changed the badge to suit the unit. He was very proud of what he achieved during his career and I think we can all empathise with that. My only reservation with Stan was why did he have to play his music so loud in the morning to wake us up for morning parades? Well at least we were never late.

Love him or hate him, you always had to respect Stan. They do not make this type of character very often, and it was a privilege to serve with him.

Read the book and enjoy.

George F. Stanford TD RLC
Lieutenant Colonel

Messages From Former TA Colleagues

Captain John Mander

'I thought I was joining a ****ing Para Unit, not ****ing Green Jackets'. With these immortal words the bargain was struck ...

Upon rejoining the ACF as an adult in 1969, I was appointed to 13 (City of London) Cadet Company, Royal Green Jackets ACF based at Sun Street. What a culture shock that proved to be, for I had completed five years as a cadet latterly with a squadron affiliated to the Royal Engineers. This had boasted fifty young men, the majority plus sixteen years, being discharged upon reaching eighteen, four years earlier, with the final rank of cadet staff sergeant. When I walked into Sun Street that evening I nearly about turned and walked out again. On parade I found one middle-aged officer, one elderly asthmatic RSM, half a dozen scruffy teenagers and ten No. 4 .303 rifles, all very clean incidentally. In fairness, much had happened in the preceding couple of years. The Regular Army, Territorials and Cadet Forces had suffered a re-organisation following an all too familiar 'defence review'. The old City of London ACF had been absorbed into one of the newly created large 'sectors' of the Greater London ACF, and to exacerbate an already fragile situation, many units with close links to the Rifle Brigade had been re-badged to the newly created Royal Green Jackets. These changes, all coming within a short time, had not been received well and many units had suffered. Over the next 18 months or so, the then OC Lieutenant (later Captain) Alex Bistoquet and I worked our socks off to improve the situation until one night a rather fierce looking character, who to my mind resembled an eighteenth century pirate [Stan had lost an eye in a work accident], turned up in answer to our prayers – and a moan about staff shortages to Sector HQ. This was Stan Scott.

Once Stan's initial misgivings about the '****ing Green Jackets, and their ****ing weird drill' had been dispelled he decided to 'give it a go' and was appointed Sergeant Major Instructor (SMI) although we always preferred a more traditional WO prefix. Some time later over a drink, yes we had a TA bar in those days – the 'team' consisting of the OC (an ex Para), Scotty and a newly appointed and pretty green 2nd Lieutenant Mander, had a 'con-flab'. It was agreed what had to be done and a cunning plan thrashed out. We immediately hit it off and henceforth SMI Scott, off parade, was universally known as 'Scotty'.

What stands out in my memory all these years later, was the sheer professionalism which Scotty exuded – the lid is opened and the memories come flooding out. The endless fights against red tape; the never ending battles against the 'heavy drill' merchants, for we were controlled by non-RGJ people in the early years; the later formation of a bugle platoon, the acquisition of a minibus, the inclusion of girls in the band, much to the dismay of County HQ, and our many later adventures.

We held numerous camps and whilst our antics were not quite in the class of Richard Sharpe's 'chosen men', they were exciting nevertheless. There were many fascinating incidents such as the 'Phantom Roman Soldiers of Colchester', Operation 'Sniggerleenni Brothers', a famous Kent-based exercise, 'Dover Sole', and the sergeants mess night when another WO nearly had a heart attack after we hid an anatomical skeleton in his bed. But of all the memories, there are two that are ingrained in my mind. The first was during an anti-tank and explosives course we attended. Scotty was faced single-handed at a range of fifty metres with a Soviet Tank, or rather a canvas mock-up, and told to fire a so-called inert anti-tank rifle grenade, already obsolete in the TA, at the target. There was a loud bang and suddenly Scotty disappeared in a cloud of smoke, dust and bits of exploding metal, as the grenade promptly blew up, destroying projectile launcher and all, but leaving the 'tank' and Scotty, who is also armour plated, intact. When the smoke had cleared Scotty casually remarked, 'I could have got the bastard with a ****ing PIAT'.

The secondly memory is Scotty's 'brew', for he could conjure up good tea, even 'compo crap' anywhere, anytime, reviving many a jaded spirit.

Stan Scott took to heart the drill and philosophy of the Royal Green Jackets perhaps because their unorthodox approach reminded him of his famous Commandos. He mastered light drill but would always wear his beloved Commando beret whilst on exercise. With the later re-formation of a Cadet Rifle battalion, then known in ACF speak as 'Group', in which Scotty played not an unimportant part, we could field 250 riflemen-like cadets with bugle platoon and drummers. But most of all it was the positive effect he had on the hundreds of teenage boys, some rogues, who passed through our ranks from the East End, Hoxton and Hackney. Many were, and quite literally in one case, saved from the clutches of the police courts. To borrow a famous phrase, we made 'damned fine fellows' of them.

In short, what can be said about a man like Stan Scott? I was proud to have served with him. It can only be imagined what fear he must have invoked in the Nazis who came up against him. What I can vouch for from personal experience, is that the sight of Stan Scott in Para smock, Commando beret and blackened face, leading an assault section charging forward firing from the hip and shouting 'Get the bastards' is a sight to behold. I know, for I was the 'enemy' up against him on many occasions and he surely put the fear of God into me. I am proud to have added my piece to this story. With Stan Scott what you see is what you get – a truly professional soldier.

Cllr. John Mander
(ITC)

Captain
OC
13th (City of London) Company
Royal Green Jackets
NE London Army Cadet Force
(Served 1969–78)

xxiii

Bugle Major Terry McCann

When a group of friends decided to try and join the Army Cadets it was a dream come true for me. From a very early age I was Army barmy and as we were aged only ten at the time and the enlistment age was thirteen, we were on a mission ! We sat down and worked out what our date of birth should be if we were the correct age and how to sign our parents' signature for the form. On the very next Tuesday we were off to Sun Street in the City of London. A Sergeant Instructor called Joe Burton met us at the door. He asked us what we wanted and sent us with a cadet to the waiting room to be seen by the Officer Commanding 13 Cadet Company No.2 Group N.E London ACF, Lieutenant John Mander. As we were taken into the office the O/C sat at a desk in front of the door, but you could not fail to miss the desk to the right at which sat the CSM, SMI Scott. To a ten year-old, he was a man mountain. His uniform was immaculate, his peak cap on the desk oozed authority. It was my first meeting with Scotty. We were found out as soon as he set eyes on us, but to him we were three kids who wanted to be there as much as he did, so he and John Mander pulled strings to get us in! So Chris Wright, Phil Morris and I joined the Royal Green Jackets Army Cadets and had some awesome adventures. We trained two nights a week under Scotty and Joe Burton, with Mr Mander running the Company. We would do map reading, weapon handling skills, field craft and regimental history. These people took young kids from the East End of London with the morals of alley cats and made them proud to be called **RIFLEMAN.** We could do things our friends could only talk of. We went away at weekends, fired real guns, took part in military exercises with other units and got camouflaged and disappeared into the undergrowth. This was where Scotty excelled. He loved to get out on the training area and tell us of his experiences during the war. His knowledge of survival skills is second to none. He would teach us how to make a shelter with nothing but what you had on you, the best place to set an ambush, what to do with prisoners, the best place to hide if you were on the run. This man was a fount of knowledge and his main aim was to give as much of it to us as possible. Scotty was a character who instilled fear in you due to his stature, but was really the big soft dad that the Scott brothers knew. I have seen his generosity towards hard-up cadets on a number of occasions but if you ask him about this he will deny it. His experience and the presence in the Company of other adult instructors inspired them to push these young kids to higher levels than the ACF thought possible. Ever the maverick, he always clashed with authority who would say, 'You cannot do this with kids'. His reply was always the same, 'They are young soldiers and I will do with them what I would do with my own kids'. He would not be told what to do by plastic soldiers. His expertise was as good in barracks as it was in the field, he was legendary on the drill square as well. He could shout the length of Saint Martin's Plain camp and still get a response.

I have tried to paint a picture of a man who was pivotal in making me the strong person I am today. I firmly believe that if the three young boys had not made that trip to Sun Street that Tuesday evening I would not be the strong, resilient, no nonsense person I am today. He does not know it but so many young scallywags from London owe him a lot. I am still in touch with some of the cadets from the early years, and whose is the name they all remember? 'Scotty'.

Bugle Major Terry McCann
Waterloo Band and Bugles,
7 Rifles.

Chapter 1

In the Beginning

Park Lane boys school, Tottenham, 1934. During the morning there had been a little bit of 'tit for tat' with a boy called Nichols, and on my way home for lunch I began to hear the sound of footsteps approaching rapidly from behind. It was him, accompanied by two cronies who duly held me against the wall while Nichols gave me a good hiding, all to the stomach because the face would leave red marks. When I got home, mum noticed my lack of appetite but made no comment. She had always said, 'Stand up for yourself. If someone hits you, kick 'em. If you can't kick 'em, nut 'em. If you can't nut 'em use your elbows, anything. Don't come home bloody crying.' My father had the same attitude. Consequently, I planned. It was obvious that the three of them could not be beaten simultaneously, so I decided to start with Nichols. Being a bully, he had made a number of enemies, which I gathered together. Knowing that he always returned to school early, I got there earlier and waited behind the school gate. As he pushed it open and began to walk up the path, the wrath did fall upon him. We ended up hanging him from a tree by his feet. His cronies were dealt with in similar fashion. After that they left us alone. This was my initiation into fisticuffs and tactics. Divide to conquer! I was ten years of age.

* * *

The Army was my father's life. Born in March 1899 and also named Stanley, he had enlisted under-age on three occasions at the beginning of the Great War, but was discharged twice due to my Grandmother informing the authorities. The third time, she said,

1

'Sod you. Stay there!' He earned the 1914–15 Star as a fifteen year old with the 10th Battalion the Queen's Own Royal West Kents, and was subsequently wounded three times. The Scott family had quite a military side to it, with my Grandfather having been in the Scots Greys, and two uncles in the Royal Fusiliers, the latter losing their lives during the First Battle of Ypres.

My parents met after the war, my mother Rose, née Whitbread, having been a munitions worker in a subsidiary of the Waltham Cross Munitions Factory along the Angel Road, Tottenham. They married in August 1922 and that same month my father enlisted into the Army Reserve. Their first child, Connie, was born in 1923 and I arrived in Henrietta Road, Tottenham on the 2 December the following year.

Mother was a big lady who had quite a temper and was simply unable to just give you a back-hander and leave it at that. She would go frantic, and by necessity I quickly learned how to dodge a blow! There was a big broom handle which I used to push the washing into the boiler and sometimes she would whack me with that. However, in the corner by the fire was a little alcove where I could hide. She would be screaming and trying to hit me with the broom handle, but only managing to bang the wall while I stoked the matter by going, 'Ho, ho, ho!' It only stopped when she tired.

Mum fed us well but could not budget money. Friday was payday and everything was always marvellous over the weekend, but by Monday it was virtually gone and the rest of the week was a scrape. Our clothes and furniture were obtained by hire purchase at so much a week and when the 'never, never' man called to collect, she would say, 'Tell him I'm out. I'll pay next week.' Sometimes, on the way to school I would take my father's suit, medals or even the carpet to the Pawn Shop. Every penny counted, and as I got older I tried to help out in various ways. I did an early morning paper round and delivered milk for Express Dairies in the White Hart Lane area. Happily, the two runs coincided, so with my little buggy, a soapbox on wheels, I delivered them all before school time. My wages totalled maybe five shillings a week. Mum took the lot. On Saturday mornings, I went to the lower Edmonton Market (The Green) and collected orange boxes, smashed them up and did a firewood round. This could earn three or four bob. Mum took the lot. I usually went to school with a mate, Dennis Essex, who lived in nearby Love Lane. Coming home one day, some houses were being pulled down, so we helped the workmen demolish walls and such-like, our reason being the profit to be made by taking the brass taps, lead water piping and any non-ferrous metals to the local scrap merchant. The same thing happened when they began building the new Tottenham Hotspur East Stand in Worcester Avenue. All this money helped the old lady.

I believe my father was ignorant of mum's problem with money. He was a driver/mechanic on buses, trolleybuses and trams for the London Passenger Transport Board (LPTB) and worked very hard, going in on rest days and doing double shifts. He often walked home after the last bus because he drove it! It was quite some distance from the depots at Wood Green and Finchley, but dad was a good soldier, he could cover ground. His only pleasures were an occasional pint and Army Reunions for the Queen's Own Royal West Kents and Royal Fusiliers. His bus pass entitled us to free rides and I had some enjoyable days out with him, visiting the West Kent's Depot at Maidstone, the Holborn Royal Fusiliers Monument and Centre, and touring round London. He taught me a lot about the Army, not the kind of information found in books, but things gained from personal experience.

The size of our family gradually increased and we had to move to larger places, firstly in Edmonton, then on to No. 2 Pretoria Road, Tottenham. By 1936 there were seven of us: Connie, myself, then brother Douglas, born in 1928, Rosemary in 1930, Gloria in '33 and subsequently twins in '36, two more sisters, Maureen and Margaret!

During that time I went to a variety of schools, but one thing never altered; the teachers were all cane-happy. Copying someone else's work, throwing ink pads, being untidy, cheeky, whispering and even not sitting up straight warranted a whack across the hands or knuckles with a ruler. More serious trouble and the Headmaster caned the seat of your pants.

Although I did all the usual things such as running and climbing, I was considered to be a little bit of a sickly boy, and so was sent to a small school called Park Lane that only had about fifty pupils. It was a new concept, 'open-air', with large fields and its own garden, ideal for any outdoor activity. A single man, Mr Norton, a saint amongst men teachers, taught all subjects including wood and metal work. I liked Geography and English but always found certain subjects boring, particularly Arithmetic. But I knew there were 240 pennies to a pound, 20 shillings to a pound, and as mum would say, 'If you can count your money and don't get swindled, you'll be all right!'

Next was Lancasterian School, Church Lane, Tottenham. I had become quite good at football, usually as a defender, but I could also play in goal, and eventually got a trial for Tottenham boys.

After a few years my brother Douglas arrived at the Primary School part of Lancasterian. He plagued me, being the big brother, because any scrape he got into it was always, 'Stanley, they're hitting me!' This wasn't so bad, but when I got home he would say, 'Mum, he's been fighting again,' and I'd get a whack from the old lady!

At around twelve years of age I moved to a new school, Sir Rowland Hill (of postal reform fame) in Lordship Lane. It was more football, more bullying. A big strong boy had a go at me and I fought him with fists, head, elbows, knees and feet, but lost, too bloody big, too strong. He didn't hit me and get away with it though, I gave him a good couple of wallops. One day a group of us were talking about him and it dawned on me that this sod was having a go at everybody. And so divide to conquer, unite to win. I had a nice little platoon of infantry and formed a plan using the ploy adopted by the Normans at the Battle of Hastings. The group met outside the local lido, next door to the school. One of the lads was sent to insult the bully and run. He chased our lad who led him straight to us. We then jumped him and belted his braces off; let's put it that way! He learned his lesson. It was not right, but you could not call a copper or go home crying. We sorted out our own troubles.

During 1938 I began to go and watch the soldiers at the newly built Engineers' Territorial Army Centre in Church Lane. The sentry at the gate would stand there holding a rifle with bayonet attached, and when it was time to be relieved, up would march another soldier and the sentry would hand over the rifle and go into the guardroom. There was one rifle between six men! With the old man having been in the Army and me being that way minded, I knew more about that rifle than they did. Sometimes I would lay there and draw it. If someone had asked me what it was, I could say, 'It's a No. 1 Mark III SMLE Short Magazine Lee Enfield, fires a .303 round, has three and a half turns in the barrel and weighs eight and a half pounds. The stud on the butt is the number of its depot. The pull-through and oil bottle are kept up the butt.' I could tell them everything about it.

Opposite the Engineers' Centre were the barracks of 'D' Company, 1/7th Middlesex Regiment, which was also a Territorial unit. One weekend I followed the Company on a route march to Epping. They kept telling me to go home, but in the end were sharing their sandwiches with me.

As I waited for my school leaving date, I heard Neville Chamberlain's announcement at home on the radio – the Second World War. Even for a kid like me, I thought, 'Here we go again, more misery.'

I subsequently went up to Church Lane to watch the Middlesex Company depart for France, and as there was no transport available, they were forced to travel in furniture lorries!

However, my only immediate interest was playing in a schools cup final versus Edmonton Boys on the Spurs Ground, quite an event. I was the goalkeeper and we won the game one–nil.

And so school days came to an end. Fourteen years of age and out into the big wide world of work. No further education.

* * *

There was no hanging about; you left school on the Friday and if lucky, started work on the Monday. I joined a tailor, Rigo's, as a seam presser. I would iron trousers, skirts, jackets, whatever; never all at the same time, always one section of this, one section of that. Unfortunately the chargehand was always on my back, a bloody lunatic. He might as well have trained in the SS. 'Come here you! You're going to iron these seams!' 'I don't want them like that, do them again.' No breaks were allowed, and one day I wanted to go to the toilet. I couldn't get permission and was not going to stand there and pee myself, so off I went. When I came back, the chargehand was standing there. 'Where have you been? What have you been up to?' I said, 'I had to go for a pee, 'cos I'm not going in my trousers,' and received a cuff round the ear. 'Don't be cheeky when I ask you a question.' I promised myself that he would not do that again. Of course, that didn't stop me from going to the toilet. On another occasion, I accidentally left the iron on the material and came back to find it burning! The chargehand came up, saw what had happened and went to bang my ear, so I ducked and his hand hit the machine. That made him angrier. Anyway, I was out, gone.

I got another job making battery cells in a factory in Commercial Road from 7.30 am until 5.00 pm, five and a half days a week. What a life for 7/6 a week. I would take home the unopened wage packet and give it to mum. She kept the lot.

Fed up with that job, I found another at Carter Patterson's in Brantwood Road, just off the Tottenham High Road. This job was really up my street because I was a 'van boy'. It was a delivery job for which you hung onto a rope on the tailboard of the vehicle, dived off with the packet, delivered it to a house, shop or whatever, got it signed for, jumped back on the wagon and away you went! The transport was an old Thorneycroft, solid-tyred lorry. My driver, Frank Dutton, taught me the morning routine of filling the radiator with water as it had to be emptied each night, how to start the engine and eventually take the lorry out of the garage and back it up to the loading bank. Frank was an ex-Cavalryman and out on the road he would recall stories about the Army. I enjoyed it. He liked a cup of tea and a bun. Our usual routine at the start of the day was to drive out of the depot, down to the first café for a cup of tea and a bun. If we went to Chingford, at the bottom of Chingford Mount was a coffee shop and it was in there for tea and a bun. If we went any other way, especially Epping, it was up the Harlow Road to another café on the left-hand side. Tea and a bun!

My favourite delivery was to a place in Buckhurst Hill, just off Queen's Road. We would deliver half a pound of butter to this dear old lady who would give me sixpence every time.

Chapter 2

Like Father, Like Son

One morning, dad had left for work as normal, but didn't come home. I was sent to find him but nobody at the bus and tram depots at Wood Green and Finchley knew of his whereabouts. I finished up at the Royal Fusiliers Centre in Holborn, and was directed to read the notices on a board. There was a list of those on the draft that had left for France that day. Dad was on it. I went home, told mum and she did her nut! Two days later we received a white envelope with green stripes around the edge, an Army envelope. It was from dad saying, 'I'm all right. I'm back in the Army and in France. You'll be getting further news, allotments and pay.' That severed relations, diplomatically and otherwise!

Between then and May 1940 he did not receive any leave. The Dunkirk evacuation passed. No dad, no news. France capitulated on the 18 June and still no news, but suddenly he was in Peterborough and the next thing, back home. He had got out of France two weeks after Dunkirk at St Malo when the second BEF was evacuated. So there was a big reunion and Sheila arrived on the scene nine months later, a 'Dunkirk baby' as we called them![1]

*   *   *

30 September 1940. Up at 5.30 am, not much breakfast, mum, five sisters and one brother all in one house, the old man away again in the Army. Here I am, a fifteen year old kid about to go to work

[1] Sheila was the only survivor of triplets, two boys, Ian and Terence. Mum had several failures, the details of which are not clear, but overall she bore sixteen children of which only those mentioned, eight, survived.

again. With the war a year old, most of my mates had gone and I was on my own. I thought, 'What did my old man do in 1914? Joined the Queen's Own Royal West Kents.' Some hope. However, nothing ventured, nothing gained. Instead of going to work, I got on a trolley bus to the Times Furnishing Store, Holloway, which had been turned into a Recruiting Office. I walked up to the big recruiting sergeant on the door. He looked at me. 'Hello, son. Do you want to join the Army?' 'Yes, Sir.' 'Where's your birth certificate and employment book?' I said, 'Do you need all that? I've just come all the way from Waltham Cross. If I've got to go home and get it all, I won't get back here today.' He said, 'Go and sit over there son.' I went over there, sat down. Other lads came in and we all went through the interview and medical. By twelve o'clock I was given my first day's pay and a railway warrant to Tonbridge to join one of the 70th Young Soldier Battalions. These battalions were for people of seventeen and a half years upward, those too young for Foreign Service but who could be used for home defence. You had to be between the ages of nineteen and forty-five to go abroad. All County Line Regiments such as the King's Royal Rifle Corps, East Kents, Essex, Suffolks, Norfolks, Sussex, had a 70th Battalion. I was in the Queen's Own Royal West Kents. Like father, like son.

The train pulled into Tonbridge Station and I walked down the hill towards the Drill Hall. I found the Orderly Room and immediately bumped into the Sergeant Major who took me to the Commanding Officer. After a few niceties and being welcomed to the battalion I was sent to the Quartermaster who gave me three scratchy blankets, a big white bag and a little white bag. These had to be filled with straw for a palliasse and pillow. Somebody said, 'Don't stuff them too much, you'll roll off!' In another part of the stores I was presented with a rifle that was thick with grease. 'You can have this. Clean it. Sign here.' And what was it? A No. 1 Mk III Lee Enfield SMLE, just like the Engineers had at Church Lane! They put me in a hut along a road called Avebury Avenue, opposite the Battalion Motor Transport garages. I got the straw, sorted out my bed and then turned my attention to the rifle. One bloke advised me to go to the garage and get a bucket of petrol to help clean off the grease. With all the prior information from the old man, I had that bloody rifle sparkling.

That night I lay in bed, tired and hungry. I did not have a tooth-brush, a bar of soap or towel, nothing, just my pillow, palliasse, rifle and civvy clothes. So ended my last day as a civilian and first as a soldier.

The next morning we received a full issue of clothing and kit, comprising a '39 pattern battledress and 08 pattern web equipment as per '14–'18 war. Although some of us had No. 1 Mk III SMLE rifles, others had the US-manufactured British P14, a horrible weapon. It was strongly made, very heavy and accurate, but only held a five-round magazine, so was no good for rapid fire. There was a long, heavy bolt that was prone to jamming. Also, when an armourer normally issues a weapon, he measures the arms of the recipient to decide which butt length to use. With the P14, it came as it was. The calibre was also .303, but it didn't matter because we had no ammunition anyway and just went through the motions of loading and unloading!

Our base for training was a cattle market in Bank Street that had been taken over by the Regiment. The cattle pens were still there and we paraded on the square in front of them.

The food was wholesome but a bit monotonous: porridge, bread and jam for breakfast, sometimes a rasher of bacon. Lunch was brown stew, tea, bread and jam, a lump of cake with a big bowl full of tea. The British Army did not issue cups at the time and these bowls were more like metal basins! Recreation was just sitting around chatting or maybe visiting the YMCA or NAAFI. On one occasion, I went for a walk along the River Medway and saw a bloke hiring out rowing boats. I liked rowing and so took one out. After a while, I noticed a plane that seemed to be heading straight for me. As it got closer I recognized it as a Messerschmitt 109 and it began to machine gun the river. I was rowing at ninety miles an hour to escape, although I think he was targeting the bridge behind me. I didn't go back to that river again!

Training continued, and after two weeks, following a route march of between ten to fifteen miles (they didn't tell us!) in the rain, we arrived back in the Bank Street area and stood at ease with our helmets on, rain capes over us, awaiting orders. However, the only order was, 'Private Scott 6352792 will report to Captain Herbert at the Company Orderly Room.' He promptly questioned me. 'How old are you Scott?' 'Eighteen, Sir.' 'Don't lie. I'll ask you again. How old are you Scott?' 'Eighteen Sir.' 'Now don't be a bloody liar, I've got a letter from your mother informing me of your real age. Hand your kit in, you're going home. Nice try, but wait a bit and try again.' I felt very dejected, but had something that a lot of people in 1940 would have liked. A discharge certificate from the British Army!

I arrived home to No. 2 Pretoria Road and walked in, only to be greeted by Connie's boyfriend, Fred Heathorn, all six feet two of him. 'Here comes England's last hope,' he said. Angrily, I answered, 'At least I didn't wait 'til they dragged me out. I VOLUNTEERED.'

My mother's first words were, 'Welcome home you silly bastard.' I just said, 'You shouldn't have done that, mum.'

* * *

Almost immediately it was back to the 7.30 am to 5.00 pm working day. I got a job at a place called Kramers in Northumberland Park Road, making ammunition boxes, banging nails in. The old boys could do it with a mouthful of nails. They seemed to spit them in. Spit, hammer, spit, hammer! The place disgusted me because every five minutes they would have a cup of tea, and all they wanted to do was play Solo. Sod the ammunition boxes was the attitude, as long as they got their wages on time.

The Blitz was in full swing and most evenings involved the same routine: arrive home from work and eat dinner, simple dishes with as much bread as possible, powdered egg, corned beef, spuds, Walton pie and tea, although not at all the same meal of course.[2]

Then we would get ready for the Anderson shelter. This meant making flasks of tea, sandwiches, getting cushions, a lamp, anything to make the night more comfortable. Buckets of water were filled (just in case), because fire was always looked upon as being more dangerous than High Explosive. There were two bunks and two chairs inside, and somehow the seven of us got in the shelter, and that was with mum being so big she took up the space of two people! When the raids started we would watch the pattern of anti-aircraft fire and learn the identifying crack of the different guns,

[2] Walton pie was made up of mostly vegetables and potato. If any pieces of meat were available at the time, these might also be included. The pie was named after the Minister of Food.

3.7 and 4.7 inch, 40 mm Bofors, and the crump of bombs, 250 kg upwards. By daytime we could distinguish between the Merlin engines of the Spitfires and Hurricanes and the Daimler Benz of Heinkels and Messerschmitts.

One night as we went to the shelter, mum said, 'Go and get some cushions.' That meant going into the big, bay-windowed front room. Opposite our house was an embankment along which the railway came out of White Hart Lane station. Connie and I were just coming out of the back door when there was a hell of a sharp screeching sound and WHACK! Behind the houses in our street were allotments, and the first bomb landed there. The next one came down between Pretoria Road and the railway, and the following one sent half the railway across the road. The next one was on the other side of the line and another landed behind the houses in the High Road. We heard later that the Anderson shelter of one of those houses was blown straight up in the air and down again. It had a family in it and not one of them was touched. A bloody miracle.

The railway was badly damaged, so the factories on the High Road side of the railway were put out of commission because the rail lines fed them. The line from White Hart Lane to Silver Street was out of action for about a week.

On another night a Molotov Basket came down roughly over the centre of our road. This was a case which dropped so far then burst open, releasing thirty-six incendiary bombs. On the corner of Pretoria Road and White Hart Lane was a fish and chip shop and a builder's yard which held wood and materials of all sorts. The incendiaries fell in the allotments, in the road, on the houses, and some in this builder's yard. I, along with Freddie Brady, our next door neighbour, got a couple of shovels and went into the yard. There were about six incendiaries spread around and we dug holes for each, putting the earth back on top to suffocate them. They were phosphorous, and so without oxygen just went out. Dig them up two hours later and they would burn again. We finished that and went back home, but in no time there was a banging on the front door. It was Freddie Brady again. 'The house up the road's on fire. Come on.' It was only six doors away. Two of the bombs had gone through the roof and we had not seen them because they were burning inside the house. We hammered on the door but could not get an answer. An old couple rented the property and we thought that maybe they were out, but somebody said, 'No, they're always there, they've got to be in there.' I opened the door using a size nine boot as a key, went down the passageway, straight into the back room and the old couple were sitting there listening to the radio, oblivious to the fact that the house was on fire! We got them away and then started to try and save some of the furniture. I was passing items out the window to Freddie in the front garden, and managed to clear the front room apart from a piano. Then Freddie said, 'You'd better get out because it's all going to come down,' so I made a sharp exit and the ruddy lot did come down. There was no way the Fire Brigade could get there because they were occupied all over the place, so the fire just burned itself out.

The following morning the house, now just a shell, was still smouldering when the actual owner of the property turned up. He looked at it and said, 'My Gawd, what a mess,' then turned around and said, 'Who put all the stuff in the front garden?' 'We did,' expecting a little thanks, but all he said was, 'You've ruined the garden!' Freddie went berserk. 'You know what you can f******* do don't you!' Freddie was a bit of a madman. During a daytime dog-fight a smoking Heinkel III came across the top of our house and we watched it go down.[3]

He was dancing in the road, shaking his arms up in the air like a lunatic, as if he had scored a goal. 'Yeah, they've got him!' He was the only bloke I ever knew act like that. Everybody else just seemed to say things like, 'They bombed Coventry last night.' 'Did they? Did they do a lot of damage?' 'Yeah.' 'Oh, what a shame.' And that was it. It was like talking about the football results sometimes. At no time did we think we would lose the war, although there was one bit of bad news that really did strike home. Next door to Freddie lived a lad called Dougie Cole. He had been seventeen and a half when, before the war, he volunteered for the Royal Air Force and graduated as a rear gunner, a very nasty job. Sadly, in November we heard that his Wellington had been shot down on a raid over Germany. His parents subsequently received news that the plane had been seen going down with the rear turret detached, falling on its own with Dougie in it.

[3] We heard later that it actually landed in the sewage farm, Sewardstone Road, down the back of Woodford.

During October I joined the local Home Guard, 'C' Company, 2nd Battalion, the Middlesex Regiment.[4]

Most of the chaps were '14–'18 wallahs who wanted to soldier, but not too much! We paraded each night at the Park Lane Drill Hall around the back of the Spurs ground. The uniforms were not the usual Army khaki material, but denim. There was a haversack, a brown leather belt, pouches that were horrible, leather gaiters and webbing which was not the normal type, but some kind of thick, waterproof, mackintosh material. The straps were poorly made, probably seconds that were not good enough for the Army but fine for the Home Guard. As the kit was so bad, people were scrounging off the Army, in fact our boots were obtained in this manner. Until they started issuing Service respirators, our civilian ones were employed. Our rifle was the P17, which was not bad, a bit heavy, all right for shooting but not for rapid fire. It fired .30-inch ammunition and as the P14 used .303, to avoid confusing the calibres, a red band was painted around the front end of the stock. There were no Lewis or Bren guns, we had American Browning Automatic Rifles, BARs. I was a bit big-headed and mentioned the time I had spent in the Army on the Lewis gun. They asked, 'You know all about these things do you?' Like an idiot I said, 'Yes,' to which they replied, 'Well you can carry the soddin' thing then!' My rifle was taken away and replaced with the BAR, and I learned to keep my mouth shut.

The Company had two 'Stand To' positions. One was a radio watch at Chestnuts Road Police Station, opposite the Tottenham Palace cinema. Our guardroom was in the cinema itself and we had to walk behind the screen to reach a little room where we could sleep. A cup of tea could be found in the Police canteen. On duty we had to go and sit by the radio for a couple of hours and wait for any signals to come through. When the telephone on the radio set beeped and a red light came on, you answered it to receive specific orders. There was a definite drill to carry out. Signal 1 was 'Stand By', Signal 2, 'Stand To' and Signal 3 meant move to an isolated house at Pickett's Lock, the position to be taken up in the event of the German invasion. To reach it we had to cross a wide, open field. Beyond the building was the embankment of the King George Reservoir, and we were facing it! One night I said to the blokes,

[4] It was Y Zone of the Home Guard.

'Here we are stuck in this house. If the Germans come over, they're going to come from behind, not from across the bloody reservoir. There's no line of approach. So how do we get out?' They said, 'You're not going to worry about running away son. You're here to stay.' I said, 'That's stupid. I don't mind fighting them, but I'm not going to stay here and die!' They just said, 'That's it.' I thought, 'What a way to think. Typical '14–'18. That's not for me, I'm going to fight and I'm going to live!'

* * *

At home one night, the sirens had gone off, aircraft had flown over and the ack-ack had blazed away, so I said to mum, 'I'd better take a walk down the Drill Hall to find out what's happening.' I walked down the street towards the railway bridge and at that point was a large bin full of grit for when the road was icy. For some reason this was a meeting point for many of the unemployed in the area and there were always half a dozen blokes standing around it, smoking and chatting. More bombers were flying over, and beyond the bridge the searchlights were up. As I passed these men one said, 'What's going on down there?' Everybody went under the bridge and looked. A parachute was descending. Somebody said, 'One of them must have baled out,' but another said, 'That ain't a bloke, that's a mine!' We watched it drift down and a debate began as to where it was going to land. It turned out to be an area called Stoney South, and a complete block of houses was obliterated. These land mines did not make big holes, but caused immense damage by blast.

And so I spent a couple of months making ammunition boxes, going through the motions with a BAR and standing guard in the Blitz.

Then enough was enough. Monday 10 February 1941. Back on the trolley bus to the old Times Furnishing Store in Holloway and believe it or not the same recruiting sergeant. 'Hello, son. Want to join the Army?' 'Yes, Sir.' 'Have you got your birth certificate?' 'No.' 'Go and sit over there.' I went and sat over there. In the afternoon I had a medical, was sworn in, nominated to the Suffolk Regiment and given a rail warrant. I went to Ipswich from Liverpool Street Station, outside which had been a bad accident and we passed a mass of railway wreckage.

Arriving at Ipswich Station that evening, we walked to the Company HQ, which was in a garage (Ripley's), then to the billet, an empty house on the Norwich Road and met the rest of the platoon. We were to be part of 'D' Company, 70th Young Soldiers Battalion, the Suffolk Regiment. I was now sixteen.

Again, big white bag, little white bag, palliasse and pillow, battle order 08 kit, '14–'18 style greatcoats, P14 rifle, Lewis guns and this time, also the French Hotchkiss gun.

We marched to our food at an old tin Mission, a Methodist Hall at the top of London Road, and trained in a Drill Hall on the Portman Road near the Ipswich Football ground. Our 'Stand To' position was a pillbox on Felixstowe Road. There was no transport.

I was in a training group again. After a while our sergeant, ex-Norfolk Regiment, said to me, 'Get your kit assembled.' I said, 'I've done it Sarge.' 'Eh?' 'I've done it. I've fitted it up, assembled all the straps and pouches, knocked two nails in the wall and hung it up.' 'Where did you learn to do that?' I gave him some waffle about my dad being in the Army. He said, 'Right, don't just sit there, get round the billet and help the others.' After a while he twigged that I had done it all before, so I told him about the West Kents and the Home Guard. That same day, everybody was fell in outside, ready to go to dinner and I heard, 'Fall out, Scott.' I fell out thinking, 'What now?' He said, 'Take them up to dinner.' So I had to march the platoon up to the tin Mission. I was acting local unpaid lance corporal, didn't wear a stripe but was the nominated man for the platoon.

The Company contained three Londoners, Watson, Higgins, both from Hoxton, and myself. The rest were all Suffolk boys. One of these locals could not march, salute, read a map, do rifle drill or even look smart. He was a sergeant's nightmare, but use a rifle? Name it and he would hit it. Being a country boy he had keen eyesight, was a good judge of distance and had a dead steady aim.

There was also a lad called Prosser, who was trying to work his ticket out of the Army by wetting the bed! He was put in the guardroom where the sentries would wake him every hour. 'Want to buy a battleship?' and he had to get up and go to the toilet. He also refused to bathe, so on a trip to the local swimming pool the sergeant and six of us got him in a bath and a good scrubbing was administered. I don't know whether it taught him a lesson, but he was still there when I left. He was not the only one who wanted out.

Another bloke was drinking Bluebell polish to try and give himself stomach ulcers. The only one to get discharged was a student who was so big that they could not find any boots to fit him. He must have taken a size 15. He went and joined the Navy!

The training continued. During one Platoon run we were in threes coming back down the road towards Ipswich Railway Station and the docks. Suddenly we heard this rumble behind us and looked up to see a Heinkel III flying just above the houses. The front gunner/bomb aimer in the nose was looking down at us and some of the boys began waving at him! And he waved back! On it went and the next thing we knew, there were huge explosions. He had bombed the dockside.

At one stage I got stuck with the job of Regimental Policeman – sixteen years old and a Regimental Policeman! My duty was in the prison with all the lads on remand awaiting trial. Some of them were my friends, so in the morning I would walk into the guardroom, and with them all banged up I'd shout, 'You dozy lot of sods,' and suchlike, while handing out fags. In that guardroom was a big inglenook fireplace in which I allowed them to sit so that all the smoke went up the chimney.

I ditched that job after a while. The regime was too brutal, too old-Army style, cleaning Dixies with water and sand, scrubbing floors, pack drill, shifting piles of sand and so on, and some of these lads were on Field Punishment for seven or fourteen days. Anything above that and they went to a glasshouse at either Fort Darlan in Chatham, or the one in Colchester.

In Ipswich there was virtually nothing to do at night, especially if you didn't have any money. On one such evening I was walking along the High Street when I passed a Community Hall and heard the sound of a young lady singing. I thought, 'That's not bad,' and went in. There were a few soldiers sitting there, most of them probably in the same situation as me. She finished the number and following sporadic applause said, 'For the next song, would one of you like to come up here and sing with me?' No one moved. She looked at me and said, 'Come on, how about you?' So I got up there and we sang *It's a Lovely Day Tomorrow*. Afterwards, I got some whistles and applause from the lads! The young lady was called Vera Lynn.

* * *

16

After finishing my time with the training group I then joined 'F' Company which was immediately sent to Nacton Aerodrome to relieve a Company of the 70th Essex Young Soldier's Battalion. This aerodrome was sometimes used as an emergency strip for planes such as Blenheims and Hurricanes. It had just suffered several days of bombing, and trees still lay across the road. The guardroom, administrative buildings and hangars had all been severely damaged. There was a factory across the road that built tank engines, radiators and similar items, so the area was a wonderful target for the Germans; if they missed one, they hit the other. Each platoon moved into an area around the 'drome and ours was in a slight valley on the western side of the perimeter. All aircraft were dispersed and we had a short-nosed Blenheim, J for Jane of *Daily Mirror* fame, as our local aircraft. The Company duties were to mount guard at the main gate, patrol the perimeter and provide night guards on two side gates, east and west. The patrols were continuous, twenty-four hours a day. The main gate guard was mounted as per Drill Book, all Blanco, Brasso, Kiwi, the stint of duty being over twenty-four hours, two on, four off. The side gate guards were mounted evening to morning, replaced at 0800 hours by a standing picket, again two hours on, four off. There would always be one more guard than was required so that a stick orderly could be chosen, this being the best presented man of that group. To be successful, attention to detail was important, because it could be decided by the inspection of the studs on the soles of your boots. The 'winner' would be given a little black walking out stick with a ferrule at one end and a silver knob at the other to signify his status, and his duty was to perform odd jobs for the Orderly Room or the Colonel, in other words act as a runner. The incentives were not having to do 'STAG' and a twenty-four hour pass.

We found the aerodrome defences to be minimal. There was an ack-ack crew with four Lewis guns and one anti-tank gun, an old French 75 mm Field piece without any ammunition. We also came across flame-thrower vehicles called Cockatrice and Heavy Cockatrice made by Lagonda Limited. These comprised a concrete pillbox mounted on either a Bedford QL 4 × 4 or AEC 6 × 6 solid-tyred chassis from former RAF fuel tender and crane lorries, strengthened with railway sleepers.[5]

[5] Sixty were built for aerodrome and harbour defence.

These lumbering nightmares could do about five miles per hour, if that, but could throw a flame a certain distance into the air vertically against dive-bombers and horizontally against ground troops.

Another defensive idea employed was to lift the tails of the aircraft and align their Browning or Vickers K guns along a road adjacent to the aerodrome.

The south side of the field was open to the Orwell River. This was covered by double apron rolls of barbed and Danet wire, all overgrown with grass and weeds. Only the rabbit runs were visible. Dawn was the time to see these animals, indeed many snares were laid to trap them. During one dawn patrol, there was myself with a P14 rifle, bayonet and five rounds and a mate with a Thompson that had a straight sixteen-round magazine (it had been found that the round ones fell off!). He was leading through the mist and suddenly began firing, so I doubled up to his side expecting trouble, but no, he was blazing away at rabbits. As .45 ammo was very scarce, he was put on a charge for negligence with a weapon. To top it all he never hit a single rabbit!

One night a badly damaged Wellington bomber with engines spluttering, limped towards the airfield and passed directly over the administrative buildings. The ack-ack promptly shot it up. However, it managed to land, and the following morning we all marvelled at how the crew had survived considering the amount of bullet holes it possessed.

We went on to do aerodrome defence at Wattisham and Martlesham bomber bases, moving from one to the other, plus a spell at the Regimental Depot in Bury St Edmunds. While there, we had to carry out a parade, all bullshit, Blanco, brass and shiny boots. Just as some General was inspecting us I saw the duty bugler exit the guardroom, draw up his bugle and sound the alarm. The parade's instant reaction was to turn right to fall out and double away to the air raid trenches, leaving the inspecting officers standing there! It was absolutely the right thing to do because it was a standing order, and to beat it all, the inspecting officer was delighted with our reaction!

We also went to Felixstowe for a two-week spell of manning the coastal positions and blockhouses. There was a switchback and on the highest area was our Observation Point.[6]

[6] Eventually part of the Butlins Holiday Camp.

During one of the nights we began to hear a throbbing noise that seemed to be coming down the coast. We listened and watched intently, but it was difficult in the dark. Suddenly a searchlight flashed into life, pointing straight out to sea, then on came another and finally a third. Sitting in the middle of these beams was a German E-boat. It was following the line of the beach, just off shore, nice and slow, and then turned out to sea, slammed its engines on and was gone. Not a shot was fired at it, not even by a bloody rifle. Those German sailors must have laughed their heads off.

We ran the fifteen miles back to Nacton, this being my introduction to the speed march. I enjoyed it. People fell out of course, but if young and fit you could hack it.

Immediately upon returning from Felixstowe I received a call to report to the Orderly Room. Such an order was always met with apprehension. 'What had I done wrong now?' The Orderly Room is the brain-box of the company or battalion, and in the Company Orderly Room you would find a Sergeant, a Corporal Clerk, the Adjutant and the Company Major. On arrival I was informed that I was being made up to lance corporal (acting, unpaid again) to act as Ration Corporal. This meant travelling to Wattisham airfield every forty-eight hours to collect the Company rations from the Ration Quartermaster. I soon got into the routine, and with there being 120 men in the Company, I always collected rations for 120 blokes. However, this baffled the Ration QM because he could not make out why no one was ever off sick, on leave or on a course. I knew he was not going to phone anybody to check the number and if he did ring the office at Nacton Aerodrome, I had primed those in the office with the answer! And so we lived like lords.

After one of these visits to Wattisham I arrived back at Nacton and finished up in the NAAFI. While drinking my tea, one of the RAF cooks started to moan about having to get up at half past three every morning to light the ovens. This had to be done to provide breakfasts for the bomber crews returning from night missions. Knowing that all the aerodrome guards belonged to my Company, I said, 'I might be able to help you there. If you supply the guard with some extra tea, coffee or cocoa and say, bacon sandwiches, anything left over from the breakfasts, I'll speak to them to see if they'll walk over in the morning and light the fires for you. They've got nothing else to do.' The guards agreed and everyone was happy.

The ration collection scheme worked extremely well until one night when I got bored. There was a pub just outside the perimeter called the Golden Fleece, and I sneaked over there for a pint. Unfortunately I had the senseless idea of walking in and out of the front gate! I was busted and the job given to someone else. Naturally, rations for the Company started to get smaller because the new bloke was informing the Ration QM of the correct number of men present. People started moaning that there was not enough to eat, and after a short period I got the job back. On seeing the QM again, I said, '120 men!' He said, 'I don't believe this. You had so many on leave last week, so many sick,' to which my response was, 'They're all back now, mate!'

The two other Londoners, Watson and Higgins, were a right couple of lads. They had the very interesting talent of being able to find things before they were lost. If you wanted something, you could have it, if they didn't have it, they 'found' it. Watson, who was short and stout, showed me how to 'bull' boots (put an extreme shine on them), and he was an expert. Higgins taught me how to pick locks with a bit of wire.

'F' Company was good. We proved it during exercises against Regular Army battalions. During one such exercise against the Gloucesters, they tried to infiltrate our position by moving through the back gardens of houses. You could fire blanks at anybody and obviously not know if you'd hit them, so we waited with bloody great clods of earth and stones, and ambushed them as they came through. The umpires, officers with white armbands were saying, 'You can't do that!' All they got was the reply, 'We won the battle mate. They're all battered and bruised. We aren't!'

On another occasion, on the other side of the aerodrome, there was an exercise with some Black Watch. We could see them forming up behind a hedgerow. Again, talk about '14–'18. Our sergeant said, 'Lads, what we are supposed to do is fire at them as they come across the open space. Then as they get near us, duck as they jump over the trench and go through. That's what we should do, but we're not going to do that. Some of you fire, the rest of you keep your heads down, and when they're halfway across that field, I'll say "UP". Get out of this bleedin' trench and go and meet them.' And that's what we did. We rushed them with bayonets fixed. The Black Watch boys didn't know what was happening, hadn't got a clue. We had our rifles at port arms and clattered into them. The Ruperts and the Rodneys (their junior and senior officer umpires) were running about like madmen. 'Stop, stop! You can't do this.' 'Rubbish, if you want a fight, have a fight. If you're going to do training, DO training!' They had battered ears, black eyes and bruises in a few other places. The 70th Battalions were all good boys. The majority of them finished up in the Airborne or the Commandos. They made some of the best soldiers in the British Army.

*   *   *

By mid-1941 the threat of invasion seemed to have died down, Jerry had invaded Russia and the only fighting was out East, Middle and Far. At home, small Commando raids cheered us up and the newspapers made much of them. Some of us decided to volunteer and went to a local place on the Felixstowe road for interviews. The first question was, 'How old are you?' 'Nineteen, Sir!' I was still sixteen. 'Can you drive? Can you swim?' The questions continued. Eventually they told us that we were all too young and to try again at a later stage.

Back at Nacton I was feeling really fed up again, and so decided to go over to the Golden Fleece for a pint. Not making the same mistake twice, this time I crawled under the perimeter wire, three rolls of it, and crossed the road. Afterwards, I returned via the same route, but just as I was about to clear the last roll of wire, my nose met two well-creased trouser legs and a pair of very shiny boots. It was the Sergeant-Major! I thought, 'I've had it this time.' 'Where have you been Scott?' 'Over the road for a pint, Sir!' He said, 'Good job you told me the truth. I saw you in there myself. Get to bed.' He was a '14–'18 veteran and a good guy.

Life went on as usual until an incident that occurred while I was on night sentry duty at a side gate. It was dark and misty and I was stood there with helmet on, respirator, rifle, bayonet fixed, but no ammunition. If German Paras began landing on the airfield, we had to go and find the Orderly Officer, who would open the wall safe to get the keys out for the safe where the ammunition was kept! Of course, we would have been dead before getting anywhere near it.

Standing there feeling cheesed off, I suddenly heard footsteps approaching from the other side of the fence. Someone was coming.

Quite an event. I saw a form, moved to the on-guard position and said, 'Halt. Who goes there?' No answer. The figure kept on coming. 'Halt. Who goes there?' Silence. The figure continued to approach. I gave a final challenge, 'Halt or I'll fire,' working the bolt as if loading. This person was now literally standing on the other side of the gate at the tip of my bayonet. It was Mrs Bennett, the Commanding Officer's wife. 'Madam, that was very naughty. You know you shouldn't do that. You're supposed to stop and answer. I could have shot you.' 'I'm Captain Bennett's wife and I want to go to the Officer's Mess.' I said, 'This gate is shut at night and you're not supposed to be here.' She said, 'This is a short cut and I can't be bothered to go around to the main gate.' At this stage I should have called out the Guard Commander and let him deal with the situation, but instead I let her through. Being a cheeky little so-and-so I said, 'Give my love to the Captain!'

Literally five minutes later the Orderly Officer arrived. 'Turn out the Guard!' The Guard turns out. 'Who is the chap who has been talking to the Company Comander's wife? I want to know or you'll all be punished.' I said, 'Don't worry. It's me.' 'Right, you'll be up in front of the Captain in the morning.' And so at 0900 hours there I was, waiting at the office. The Sergeant-Major looked at me and said, 'What have you been doing?' I told him. Into the Company Commander's office I went, 'Quick march, lift, rite, lift, rite, halt. Lift turn.' Now this was unusual, because when someone was on a charge his belt and hat were removed and he was then marched in with an escort, but none of this had happened. The Captain said, 'Leave us Sergeant-Major and shut the door behind you.' He then laid into me in Swahili, Chinese, Zulu and other languages, calling me everything from Newcastle to Exeter and finished by saying, 'You are insolent. If I had my way I would take off my jacket and give you a good thrashing.' I said, 'Go on then, try it and see what a lad from Tottenham can do!' Thereupon he had a blue fit. I knew he couldn't do anything. It was personal, his wife was in the wrong and I should not have been alone in his office. He screamed for the Sergeant-Major, 'Get him out of my sight.' Outside, the Sergeant-Major asked, 'What the ruddy hell did you say to him?' When I told him he said, 'Gawd blimey! Get out of it and pronto!' I went back to my block, sat on the bed and thought, 'Sod this crowd.' I got a sheet of paper and wrote out a request for a transfer back to the West Kent

Regiment. It had not been in the office half an hour when a railway warrant and the rest of the day's rations appeared. Pack your bags and get! Twenty-four hours later I found myself back home with 'C' Company, 4th Battalion, Queen's Own Royal West Kents at Deal near Dover. I thought it was the best thing I had ever done in my life.

Although the 4th was a Territorial Battalion, it was a front-line unit, having fought in France, coming back via Dunkirk, having had a good go at Jerry during the retreat.

The morning after arrival there was an interview with my new Company Commander. The first thing he said was, 'Welcome to "C" Company. Are you a sportsman?' 'Sir?' 'Do you play soccer?' I said, 'I play football!' 'Do you box?' 'I have boxed a bit with the Suffolks.' 'Good, good, good. There is a football trial tomorrow. We've got a game and you can play.' So I found myself in the Company team, and after an inter-Company football tournament, ended up playing for the Battalion. The relevance of this was that all of the sportsmen went into the 'Battle Patrol' as they called it, a little like a group of Commando soldiers. We had to wear cap comforters and blacken our faces like the big boys were doing.

The barracks were in a school on the north side of town and the Company would run from there to Betteshanger Colliery in brown plimsoles, denim trousers and cap comforter, with towel and soap wrapped up in a pack. On arrival we would hang our gear on the hooks, have a shower and get cleaned up. Then get dressed again and run all the way back to Deal! We returned in a dirtier condition than on arrival at Betteshanger. What was the sense in this? No one knew. There was only one answer. It was the British Army!

From early 1942, life was settled. The Company trained hard and played football, and I started my courtship with the Bren gun. The unit moved to Otham, outside Maidstone, for some three-day exercises and then on to Kingswood to finalize the battle training. Shortly after, we were informed that the Battalion was going over-seas, to the Middle East. We then had to test our weapons, paint our brasses so that they didn't glow, stop blancoing the kit, and get inoculated for TB, Tet and so on. New NCOs arrived. One I will never forget, Prossen, a big corporal, who walked in the room and you knew instantly that he was an experienced soldier. There was an air about him, no nonsense. He asked us, 'Are any of you willing to die for your country?' One of the blokes replied, 'I suppose so,

Corp.' He said, 'Bloody idiot. Stay alive for your country. Let the other sod die!' I thought, 'That makes sense!'

We received some embarkation leave, but when I got home I was greeted with the usual questions. 'When are you going back?' and 'What have you got?' because everybody was on the scrounge. Anything you could pick up was taken home and that's what they used to look for. From my mother, it was the ration book and the money. Where was all this family joy and happiness to see you at home? I would go out, lollop about, get bored and if I had a week's leave, nine times out of ten, after about four days I would return to the barracks. They would ask, 'What are you doing back here?' 'Fed up, so I came back.' What was the good of staying at home? Nothing there.

When everybody returned from leave, we were informed that the next morning everything was to be nice and neat because the King was going to inspect the Division. We therefore had to scrape the paint off, then re-polish the brass, re-blanco the gear and press our trousers. What a game. The next morning at 0530 hours, our Brigade, 132, was on the road at Sutton, near Kingswood. The whole 44th Home Counties Division was lining one road. We were stood there until 1030 hours when finally, along came a convoy. An armoured car, motorbikes, military police with several other vehicles, and in one of them was King George VI waving a hand. I had a good look and thought, 'He's got bloody powder and make-up on!' I couldn't believe it. Then more motorbikes, more cars, more armoured cars and away he went. All over. At 1100 hours we marched back to our billets and at midday were told to repaint our brasses, clean our weapons, carry out the whole bloody routine again.

Then came the bombshell. 'When the Battalion moves out, these people are nominated for the rear party.' Well, 5835939 Private Scott was on it. I was absolutely gutted. I was happy in the Company and had made many friends, but there was nothing I could do about it. The Battalion set off for North Africa and I missed out again.

I had to report to 132 Brigade HQ. The three infantry battalions of the Brigade had all been supplied with new equipment and so their old kit was placed in the respective battalion store. From there, it was sent to Brigade HQ where the task of the rear parties was to sort, package and send it all to the depot at Aldershot, boots, shirts, blankets, everything.

The Quartermaster's Store was a soldier's paradise, and I picked two nice pairs of boots, two well fitting battledresses and changed all my other kit for items that fitted and were in good condition!

Being an acting unpaid lance corporal yet again, I was ordered to take a lorry load of blankets to Aldershot. We had to go through Guildford and while travelling along the Hog's Back the driver asked, 'Corp, I don't live far from here. Couldn't nip home for a cup of tea could I?' I said, 'You've got your route, stick to it.' We went on a bit further and he said, 'It wouldn't take a minute to nip home for a quick cup of tea. I could see the missus.' I thought, 'Oh yeah, I get the cup of tea, you have a short session with the missus!' In the end I said, 'Go on then.' So we parked outside his house and bowled in. I received a better reception in that house than when I went home. His wife said, 'Hello mate, come in, sit down and have a cup of tea,' and I was given a lump of cake as well. They went upstairs and his father, an old soldier, started talking to me about the way things used to be, and then asked what I had in the lorry. 'We're taking a load of blankets back to Aldershot.' 'Cor, blankets. Are they the same as we used to have in '14–'18?' 'I suppose so.' 'Do you know what, they're worth ten bob each. You can't get blankets now you know, with the clothing rationing.' The driver never did get a cup of tea and when we left, a roll of ten blankets had fallen off the lorry and I had a fiver in my pocket! Arriving at the depot the bloke in charge just said, 'Dump them over there.' He didn't care about the paperwork. I could have flogged half the lorry off and it wouldn't have mattered. I was a naughty boy I suppose but wasn't the only one. The NAAFI manager at the base mentioned that he could do with a pair of Wellington boots because there was a load going back to the depot. I said, 'My family could do with some chocolate.' That was the name of the game with rationing going on. The next time I went on leave I took home Cadbury bars. The British soldier does not loot or steal, he scrounges.

Finally, to follow up the Battalion we had to go to the Regimental Depot at Maidstone. I decided to go home for one last weekend. Bomb damage had forced us out of Pretoria Road, and initially a place was provided in Victoria Crescent, but it was an appalling, rat-infested hole, so the family was moved to No. 41 Grove Road, Tottenham.

I got off the train at London Bridge and fell foul of the Military Police. 'Come here soldier. Where's your pass?' I hadn't got one and so made a run for it and escaped. On the return journey I dodged them again, but then walked straight into some others. I was taken down to Scotland Yard and stuck in a cell. The battalion was contacted and a sergeant came up with two blokes to get me out. Handcuffed to the sergeant I was marched out of Scotland Yard under the guard of rifles with fixed bayonets. I felt like a criminal, yet there were thousands of servicemen without passes doing the same thing each week. They walked me to Trafalgar Square where the sergeant took the handcuffs off and said to the guards, 'Take those bayonets off. Come on, we're going down the Underground.' He took us to his mother's place at Swiss Cottage! When we got there he told her what he was doing and she kept looking at me and saying, 'Naughty boy, tut, tut, tut!' We were supplied with lumps of chocolate cake and iced coffee, which I had never drunk before in my life. I thought, 'Where does she get it all from?' Afterwards, we headed down to Charing Cross Station and found a train going back, but it was completely full. The sergeant said to the escort, 'Put your bayonets on. Stand there.' He went down to the office, came back with a Royal Engineer who was the Railway Transport Officer, and said, 'Here I am with prisoner and escort and I've got to have a place to myself. This bloke is dangerous!' The RTO opened a compartment door and said to the occupants, 'Get out, everybody out.' Moaning and groaning, they all got off. We got on and the RTO officer locked us in, saying, 'I'll warn them at the other end to come and unlock the door.' So we had one guard in each corner and me and the sergeant at the other end. All the comfort in the world! Reaching the other end, the door was duly unlocked and we walked out.

Consequently, I went up in front of the OC who said, 'I don't know what to do with you. Take an admonishment,' and that was it. But then what followed half destroyed me as a soldier. They had formed a draft to go and reinforce the 2/7th Queen's, the 2nd of Foot (Mutton Lancers),[7] and put me on it. The Queen's Royal Regiment was not a bad one, being the oldest English infantry regiment in the British Army, dating back to 1661, but definitely not Scotty's cup of

[7] So called because of their cap badge which features a lamb and a lance.

tea. I was moaning like hell, 'I'm a West Kent man. My old man was a West Kent Man, my uncle was a West Kent man. I'm not going to wear that bloody badge!' However, there was no choice of course.

I had to report to a place called Chadacre Hall near Lavenham, south of Bury St Edmonds, to join 14 Platoon, 'C' Company, as a Section Bren Gunner. I didn't like it at all and ran foul of them straight away. It was always, 'I'm on guard tonight Scotty. Lend us your trousers, boots or webbing.' Anything for guard they called, 'mucking in'. I called it slovenliness. I would help a man get ready, but lend him my kit? No way. In the West Kents and the Suffolks, each man had been a self-contained unit, which meant he had everything of his own, from bootlaces to cap badge. He looked after it, cleaned it, polished it. I was like that. If you were foolish enough to lend anything, you would probably get it back in poor order. I said, 'No,' and so was not in the 'clique'. This refusal brought forth animosity. My main antagonists were a Sergeant 'Granny' Barnard and a Private Frost. They didn't like me and I didn't like them. Frosty and I often shared knuckles. I couldn't even look at him! If he walked up the passageway while I was coming the other way, he would not give way and neither would I. That was it. I always said, 'You can hit me if you want, but then stand there and take what you're going to get back. That's how it is.' 'Granny' Barnard found fault wherever he could. Every so often, the Company would do all the Battalion duties like fire pickets, patrols, guards. There were only 'A', 'B' and 'C' Companies in a Battalion, the rest was HQ and specialists, signals and so forth, but the rifle companies did the duties. So Duty Company came round every four weeks and during our week I would have fire picket, patrol, guard, then back on fire picket. It used to come round more than enough. I was no slouch, but being only seventeen, it really hurt. However, some of the guys like Corporal Jeffreys and Lance-Corporal Allen were OK and did more than enough to level things up.

Then I was cheered up. News arrived that we were going overseas!

Chapter 3

Overseas – At Last!

The Battalion proceeded to Liverpool and embarked on a big Dutch troopship, the *Johann Van Olden Barneveldt*. We subsequently sailed up to Greenock and formed part of a convoy heading for Freetown, West Africa. The North Atlantic was very rough and everybody was seasick, but eventually we crossed the line, and the weather became very hot. Below decks it stank, particularly near the heads (WCs). Saltwater soap was provided to wash with, but it was awful. There was no lather, it just covered you in a kind of white slime. Daily training was PT, first aid, signals (semaphore), other lectures and of course, inspections ('rounds' in the Navy).

'Granny' Barnard continued in the same fashion. 'Scott, you're on watch.' We reached Cape Town, real civilization (unless you were black), and were given four days shore leave. Everyone was warned about getting drunk because spirits were far cheaper than beer. A mate and I walked out of the dock gate and headed for a pub we had been told about called The Queen's. On our way a big open-topped car pulled up beside us and the driver asked, 'Excuse me, are you going for a drink?' Of course our first thought was, 'What the hell has it got to do with you?', but he then started to give us a lecture about what to expect in The Queen's and finished by saying, 'Why don't you come over to my place and have a drink there?' Putting aside our doubts about this offer, we decided to give it a go. He drove us to an area between the Lion's Head and Table Mountain and pulled up outside a house with a front garden the size of Hyde Park. His wife and two young daughters made us very welcome and we were suddenly sitting in the garden drinking iced lemonade. They asked how long we had got in Cape Town and after we told them the father said, 'You can stay with us for the four days. Don't worry about going back to the ship.' So that night I went back to see the Company Commander and he gave us permission. During those remaining few days our hosts took us to Elizabeth Bay with its crystal clear water and then up Table Mountain for a night-time picnic. With the food and way of life, for us with our background, this short period was out of this world. Afterwards they drove us down to the dock and waved goodbye.

We then sailed around the Cape to the mystic Orient, Bombay. What an aroma! Unwashed bodies. The Battalion marched to Colaba Transit Camp for yet more training, and while here I got to know many of the wallahs such as the char (tea) wallah and dhobi (laundry) wallah (watch out for the loose wallah, the thief). After a short stay there was a Battalion parade during which the Camp Commandant, a Colonel in the Duke of Wellington's Regiment gave us a 'talk'. While he was giving us this 'talk', an aeroplane was buzzing around and every time he reached a certain part of his speech, it droned over. In the end he stopped and said, 'Has anybody got an anti-tank rifle? Shoot that poxy aeroplane down!' Where did he come from? An anti-tank rifle!

Embarking on another Dutch troopship, the *Nieuw Amsterdam*, we sailed up the Persian Gulf to Basra. It was the cesspit of cesspits. The Battalion disembarked, climbed onto lorries and proceeded out into the desert towards Shieba. What a ride. Dirt, dust and flies. Miles into the hinterland, the ship could still be seen, as if it was sitting on the sand. We arrived at Point X, the camp for the 56th London Division to which the 2/7th Queen's belonged. There was one waterhole and out of our Brigade, 169, the Queen's got it, 'C' Company got it, then 14 Platoon and yes of course, Scott got it. 'You're on guard at the waterhole.' 'Good, bags of water!' WRONG. It was shuttered, bolted and locked. Water was rationed, and issued every morning.

Next was training, or acclimatization as it was referred to, in order to get us used to the heat, dust, storms and flies, as we expected to join the 8th Army in North Africa. We were camped in ten-man tents, each soldier having his own little area. Everyone's personal mosquito net was hooked to the roof of the tent. Once inside the net, you sat there for a few minutes to kill any mosquitoes that were already there. During this period some people got dysentery and sandfly fever, which was worse than malaria. The sandfly was a red pin-sized insect, more like an ant than a fly, and it could get through the net. Its effect was staggering. One night a bloke started screaming and began to have what seemed like a fit. Eight of us had to sit on him while the other one went for the medic.

Eventually we moved by train to a nice little place called Kirkuk. The train was cramped and the journey very uncomfortable. At Baghdad there was no railway bridge, so everyone had to get off and lug their kit north of the river while the train was ferried over. Then it was back on the train. As we reached Kirkuk it was teeming with rain, and the Division took up a site, unit by unit, along the Kirkuk–Mosul road (the only one). When a Division is set out, all of the soft-skinned vehicles are placed at the back or in the middle, with the infantry battalions around the outside to protect them. 169 was of course the last Brigade to take up position, the 2/7th Queen's the last battalion of the Brigade, 'C' Company was naturally one of the last Companies, and so 14 Platoon one of the last platoons on the perimeter. Consequently we were nearest the local population, the Kurds.

Then it started again. Field training, guards and patrols. A small arms competition was held which I won, and went with high expectations to see the Colonel, Bols, for my prize. To my amazement it was a blue airmail envelope to write home with!

Kirkuk was an oil centre, a pumping station to Haifa, and part of our job was patrolling the oil line. The other part was chasing the Kurds. They would steal anything and had been doing this in the area for some time. As the whole Division was strung along the road, the local tribes would just come down and raid wherever they wanted. To ensure that we didn't lose our weapons, each night we had to dig a groove in the ground, wrap our rifles, place them in the groove and then sleep on top.

After one raid, Intelligence told us that they came from the local village, so with 'C' Company being the duty Company for that period, we had to go out in battle order to this spot. Troops were placed to cordon off the area and I got down in position on a slight rise and could see the entrance to the village. The platoon sergeant, said, 'Load.' Magazine on, gun ready, safety-catch off. 'If you get the order to fire, see that roof? Hit it!' This was to the right, on a house built with sun-baked mud, though the roof seemed to be red slates.

31

The troops went in and there was a bit of a humdrum, then all of a sudden the voice behind me said, 'Bren, FIRE!' There are twenty-eight rounds in a Bren magazine and you are supposed to fire in five round bursts. Bullshit. If you are going to hit somebody, hit them. I just let it have twenty-eight rounds. Woooffff, gone. The result surprised me because the whole roof seemed to disintegrate. I had to stop because the working parts of the Bren stay to the rear when the magazine is empty and I didn't get a chance to reload before the order came to cease fire. That was that. Three empty three-ton lorries were driven into the village and came out full up. They found weapons, blankets, you name it, it was there.

When off duty there were one or two things you could do. There was a cinema on the road out of Kirkuk called the K1, where we saw all sorts of French, Yank and British films, but with English, French plus Arabic subtitles at the top, bottom and sides of the film! The Kurds sold us such things as oranges and egg sandwiches. The lads bought the sandwiches, ate the egg and threw the bread away. The Kurds duly picked it up, dusted it off and put a new egg in! Fair enough, we sold them used tea leaves, so it was give and take!

Christmas 1942 approached, and for the dinner the Quartermaster had somehow got hold of a large amount of mangy chickens, probably by buying them off the Arabs. A fatigue party was formed to wring their necks, and I happened to be one of them. Some of the blokes were going the wrong way about it, pulling their heads straight off instead of wringing their necks. After killing them they had to be plucked and the guts removed by sticking your hand up their rear. Not a very nice job. A chicken should not be plucked when it has just been killed, it's better to wait a while. It is the same as killing a pheasant, the body has to be allowed to cool because each feather has got quite an amount rooted in the body. Usually it is hung up for three or four days to make the feathers easier to pluck, but Army people are impatient. 'Kill 'em, pluck 'em, get 'em ready for the cook.' God knows how many necks had to be wrung, but I got sick of the sight of bloody chickens, although they were quite nice when we ate them!

After our Christmas dinner the Division went straight out on an exercise. There was a Jock in our platoon who had red hair and sideburns down past his ears. He was told time and time again to shorten them, but never would. Eventually they were growing under his cheekbones! After the first night on exercise we dug in and brewed up. Jock said, 'It's Christmas and we haven't got a drink.' Well, he did get a drink because our platoon officer had a bottle of spirit for a cooker. Jock managed to get hold of this bottle, and I've known Scots drink some funny things, but methylated spirit? In the morning the Battalion moved on, 'C' Company moved on and 14 Platoon moved on, but we left Jock buried under three feet of sand. It was all we could do for him.

The three-day exercise entailed crossing the Euphrates and Tigris rivers. The engineers built a Pontoon Bridge over the Tigris, which was swollen due to the winter rain and wind. A Quad, a British Army tractor with a 25-pounder gun and a limber, went across, and whether the bridge was right or wrong I don't know, but it tilted and the whole lot went straight in the drink. About four gunners were drowned. Another accident occurred when a bloke called Phillips was shot straight through the head by friendly fire.

On the last day of the exercise, we were in the Kurdish foothills to the rear of the camp. Beyond those mountains was Iran. We had been slogging for the whole exercise. I was a young man, not yet eighteen and had been lugging the Bren gun, four magazines in my webbing, all my kit plus utility pouches that held another six magazines. So ten Bren gun magazines, twenty-eight rounds per magazine, that's 280 rounds of ammo, and it weighed! By the end of the three days I was on my bloody chinstrap, as were the others, and we still had a long march over the foothills back to the camp. The foothills were up and down, the roads stony and it was hot. I began to fall further and further back, still slogging but having slowed right down. I had no intention of stopping because letting the Kurds get hold of you didn't just mean death, it meant mutilation. You knew that they were watching all the time, you could almost feel it. In the end the Company Commander detailed 'Granny' Barnard to stay behind and keep me going, which he did by continually kicking me up the arse and smacking me round the earhole. 'Get on, you bastard.' Eventually I realized that Barnard wasn't worried about me, he was shit scared for himself. On that day I promised myself, 'If I see him outside the Army, the first thing I'm going to do is smash him in the mouth!' And I meant it.[8]

Another of our duties was to mount guard at an RAF bomb dump situated in the foothills. The bombs were just sitting in the open with no cover at all. During our first guard duty an RAF water tender arrived, two men got out, fixed a hose on the back and started hosing down the bombs. It was so hot that they were sizzling. We asked, 'What's the idea of doing that? It's a waste of water,' and got the response, 'Well, if we don't do it, there's an outside chance they might explode!' They then packed up and left, leaving us alone with that thought, which we subsequently had in our minds for each stint, two hours on, four hours off and then back on for another two hours. Not a nice feeling!

Around January 1943, whispers began about a move to join the 8th Army in North Africa, and for me not before time. Some people

[8] I eventually got that chance in about 1998. I received a letter from the 2/7th Battalion Queen's Royal Regiment Old Comrades Association inviting me to the Pembury Arms in Pimlico for a reunion dinner. I phoned the secretary, introduced myself and said, 'Would a certain person called ex-Sergeant Barnard be there?' He said, 'Wait a minute,' checked the list and said, 'Yes, he'll be there.' I said, 'Good, I've been waiting since 1943 to see him!' The secretary said, 'That's nice, what for?' I said, 'I'm going to smack him straight in the gob!' At the dinner I was one of the first people there because I was waiting on him coming through the door. I don't know what happened, whether this secretary warned Barnard that a certain bloke, name of Scott, was looking for him, but he never turned up.

A year later, again, the reunion. I thought I'd try it once more. I got down to the Pembury Arms quite early and was standing at the bar having a drink, when in walked this geezer. I looked at him and thought, 'That's him!' He walked over to the bar, ordered himself a drink and looked at me. He said, 'Are you here for the reunion?' I said, 'Yes.' He said, 'Do I know you?' I said, 'Yes, you do, and I know you, but I don't think you remember me, because the last time I saw you I made myself a promise. Now come over here.' I took him over into the corner and said, 'That promise was, Sergeant Barnard, that the next time I saw you I'd smack you straight in the gob! But looking at you, if I hit you, you'd fall to pieces.' He was in a pretty bad way. 'But now I've seen you and told you, that's it. By the way, my name's Scott and I was in your platoon. Maybe you'll remember now,' and walked away. During the dinner, the waiter came up with a drink. I said, 'Where's this from?' 'The gentleman down there told me to bring it to you.' I looked and it was Barnard. I said, 'Tell him he can put his beer where he's got his haemorrhoids!' So that was that. It was a good mob the Queen's, a lot of bullshit, but just maybe I fell into a bad Company, like 'C' Company or a bad platoon, like 14 Platoon. I've not said thank you to that battalion and I never will.

said, 'Hey, stupid, slow down,' but the war was in Egypt and we were playing silly buggers chasing Kurds in Northern Iraq. I wanted to use my Bren gun for its purpose. Most people around me were National Service. I volunteered, too young to know better I suppose, but that was it, get into action and find out what it's all about. Unfortunately, after all this time, somehow my real age had again been discovered. I think it may have been something in a personal letter sent to me by my mother and elder sister. And so it was, 'Go back to Baghdad where you will find the 4th Battalion Q.O.R. West Kents doing Ambassador Residence guard and then England.' There was a bloody war on and they were sending me home.

So while I packed my kit, the 2/7th Queen's and 56th Division went to Libya. I was given an old P14 rifle and 500 Victory V fags by the QM and a rail warrant to Basra, via Baghdad. I hitched a lift by lorry to the Kirkuk railhead and got on the train, and chumming up with two 'erks' from the RAF, we moved into the last wagon, laid our bed rolls down and rested. Travelling south there was endless desert. The train was wooden, draughty and so slow that we could get off and run up to the engine, cadge some hot water, wait for the last wagon, hop back on and make tea! Food-wise, we lived on biscuits and a 7 lb tin of corned beef.

And so on to Baghdad where we threw the rest of the tinned bully away, only for it to be pounced upon by half a dozen Arabs. We entered the North station, detrained and moved to a transit camp for forty-eight hours. My old battalion, the 4th West Kents was actually camped outside the town, but I was able to hitch a lift to see them. I found they had been severely mauled during Rommel's assault on the Alamein position. A friend of mine, Kenny Brett, and a few others including my ex-Platoon officer, Lieutenant Watney had been killed at Alam Halfa. The time soon passed and it was back on the train to Basra and a transit camp until we boarded a Polish ship, the SS *Kosciusko* and a more rusty, stinking bucket you could not wish to find. The crew was mostly Lascars, but with some Londoners. Lascars were native seamen from such places as India, Java, Indonesia and they were good hands who worked well. I was told not to watch them while they were preparing their food as it was something to do with their religion. But being a nosey little sod, one day, while in the Persian Gulf, I went and stood on a short ladder with my head just above the fore-deck to watch them. They were cooking on spits over a charcoal fire. One bloke made chapattis. When ready they held the chappati in one hand, laid the meat and everything else in the middle, pulled the skewer out, flopped the chappati over and over, and ate it long-wise. Of course, one of them saw me, came over and said in his pidgin English, 'You watch? You look?' I said, 'Yes,' thinking, 'I'm in bother again.' But he said, 'You like?' 'Me like? Yes,' and he took me up there. I squatted down around the fire with the others and explained that I was not just being nosey, I was interested and liked to see how other people did things. They gave me some of this food and it was quite nice. I got on well with them and there was no trouble at all.

After a fifteen-day journey back to Bombay, I was sent ashore to the Colaba transit camp. I should have been provided with certain pieces of documentation but due to some administrative error, nothing could be found. When I reached the camp, I had to report as a new arrival, and when I said I didn't have any papers and where I had come from, they thought I was a deserter. I was immediately put behind bars! Big Indian soldiers stood guard on the gate. I was soon bored out of my brain, so after a while I pulled a jack knife out of my pocket and started pruning my nails. One of the sentries then saw the knife and a major alarm ensued! Rifles and bayonets were pointed at me until they came in and took it away. After spending the night there, I was called over to the office again. The officer, the same Colonel from our previous visit, Duke of Wellington's Red Socks, said, 'We've got your papers from the ship, but I don't know what to do with you.' So he gave me thirty-one days leave, pending repatriation to England.

Colaba Camp was quite good. There was a human Sergeant-Major who spoke to you, a cook who knew how to cook and friendly sepoys. But what does a young soldier do in Bombay? There was nothing there. I would take a shower in the morning, go down to the beach, into the sea and out. Come back to the camp, have lunch, take a shower, go down town. There was a cinema where I saw two films, one was *Gone with the Wind*, and the other was about how the gallant Yanks fought off the Japs at *Wake Island*. Other than that it was walk around from one British Army canteen to another. After sixteen days of utter boredom, the Sergeant-Major said, 'Scott, pack your kit lad, you're on a boat in the morning.' I went back to my tent, sat on the charpoy, the Indian bed made of eight pieces of wood and a lot of rope, packed my kit and sat there all night. I dared not move!

At dawn we were formed up in front of the office and the Duke of Wellington's officer came out and gave us a lecture about marching smartly through the town. Someone said, 'Get a bloody move on, we'll miss the boat!' He stood there and went pink! He threatened to stop us going if the man didn't own up, but no one did. In the end he gave up and away we went. We marched down the Holborn Road, through the Yellow Dock gates to the dockside, sat down and waited. And we waited and we waited. We must have sat there for around five hours until approximately one o'clock when the Lighters started coming in to take us out to the ship. We found that it had been worth the wait because it turned out to be HMT *Mauretania*! A lovely, big, fast, modern, two-funnelled English liner, so it was unescorted. Previously, it had been transporting Yanks and so there were Coca-Cola and iced water machines around the decks, the canteens were selling Lucky Strike and Phillip Morris fags, half a crown for a carton of 200. The food was good and the ship was not overcrowded. She had her own guns and a request was made for people who could handle them, so I volunteered to be a machine gunner. My position was up on the starboard wing of the bridge, with twin Lewis guns. These had not been cleaned since New York and were covered in salt, so before anything else that had to be done, but it gave me something to do. From Bombay we sailed to Madagascar, Diego Suarez, then around the Cape of Good Hope to Cape Town. There were four days shore leave but unfortunately I did not get to see our South African friends again. The most memorable moment was when a mate and I were walking along and a very nice young lady asked if we would like to go with her. We thought our luck had changed and so followed her, but ended up in an old Mission with a cup of tea and a bun! As a thank you we had to sing a hymn in return! Then it was off again to Freetown, crossing the line for the fourth time. In Freetown we picked up survivors from the *Empress of Canada*, which had been torpedoed. The ship had been carrying families of time-expired soldiers from India, Italian prisoners of war and some Poles who had been released by the Soviet Union after the German invasion. After the first torpedo had struck, the submarine surfaced and proved to be Italian. The *Empress* was hailed and informed that so much time was being given to abandon ship. The submarine then submerged, went round to the other side of the ship and slapped in another torpedo. Several of the British survivors told me that instead of helping the women and children and letting the prisoners out from down in the holds, many of the Greek crew were the first ones over the side into the boats. When the Italians were released, it was they who had helped the families get into the lifeboats and away. And so, when the Italian survivors boarded the *Mauretania*, although they had to be put in the hold, we made sure they were well treated.[9]

A request was made over the tannoy for volunteers to help care for these women and kids, so I got involved in getting their food, keeping the kids happy, anything you could do to help.

[9] The *Empress of Canada* had left Durban on 1 March 1943 with about 1,800 people on board. On the night of 13–14 March 1943, the ship was torpedoed twice by the Italian submarine *Leonardo da Vinci* about 400 miles south of Cape Palmas and sank within 20 minutes after the second attack. There were nearly 400 fatalities.

Chapter 4

Back in Blighty

The *Mauretania* docked at Liverpool on 9 April 1943. Our reception committee on the quayside was two Red Caps, and of course they got a nice cheer. When I disembarked I had virtually no Army gear. The P14 that the Quartermaster had given me in Iraq went through the porthole as we came up the Mersey because I didn't want to carry that load of rubbish about. Naturally I still had my kit bag – it was stuffed with cans! Any space I could make was packed with food that I got on the ship. The large pack on my back was filled with fags. The group of soldiers with whom I had become friendly were mostly time-expired regulars, so I was the youngest one amongst them. We were put on a train and sent straight down to Hythe in Sussex, to the 15th Holding Battalion of the Queen's and spent a week going through kit inspections, medical check-ups and such-like. Then the Quartermaster came round to check what we had got against what we should have had. Of course it was the usual Army drill. 'Two pair of boots?' 'One'. 'Three pair of socks?' 'One'. 'Three shirts, three undershirts, three pants?' 'One!' Then they took the numbers of your weapons; 'Where's your weapon?' 'Ain't got one.' 'Why?' 'Out there I was a Bren gunner and I had to hand it in when I came home.' One of the group said, 'There's a war on out there mate. They need the weapons there, not here!' After the week-end we were sent on leave. I got home, banged on the door, but there was no answer. Old Mother Parsons, the next door neighbour, must have heard me, as she came out and said, 'There's nobody at home.' She talked as if I was a total stranger, didn't recognize me at all. 'Who do you want to see?' 'I'm Stanley!' At that moment, she looked around the hedge, down the road and said, 'Your mother's just coming up the road.' I looked round and there was mum, Connie, Rosie, and young Sheila in a pushchair. Rosie spotted me, screamed, 'It's Stanley!' and there was the charge of the Light Brigade up the road. It was 'Welcome home,' and all that sort of thing. We got indoors and while mum put the kettle on, they were all sitting there in the corner, waiting. The usual questions began: 'How long have you got?' 'When are you going back?' and 'What have you got in the bag?' I opened the bag and out came tins of bacon, beans, peas, jam, bars of chocolate, packets of Lucky Strike and Phillip Morris. Tobacco and cigarettes were in very short supply. They thought it was Christmas, especially as the rationing in 1943 had been very tough.

I had been given fourteen days leave, but as usual, was back with the unit within seven.

I was posted to a Holding Battalion in Redcar, Yorkshire, and yet again started training! We were in an old school on the south side of Redcar, not far from the beach. While there, one night a lone Jerry raider came over the beach, dropped a couple of bombs and must have wondered what the hell had happened because the whole minefield went up, one setting off another, right the way along the beach.

In town was a pub called The Bricklayers where before getting the chance to sit down, someone gave you a drink. It was not like the pubs in southern England where you walked in and everyone ignored you. And it was no good saying, 'My round,' because they would tell you to 'Shut up and sit there.' Opposite the school was a fish and chip shop run by an old lady. Every tenth customer got their fish and chips for nothing. That was how those people were.

The highlight during this period was doing a 'Salute the Soldier' week in Middlesborough. There were also 'Salute the Sailor' and 'Salute the Airman' weeks, parades and fetes to raise funds for, in this case, the Army Benevolent Fund. We parked our lorries in a side street, got on parade and formed into four 3-inch mortar teams. A team was a minimum of four men, numbers 1, 2 and 3 to set up the weapon and 4 to bring up the ammunition. There was also of course the man who controlled you. We were in two ranks, eight and eight behind, the people commanding, in front. Having just come back from the Middle East, we were brown, tanned, not like the weenies behind us, all white-faced! We marched through just as they do in a carnival, came back to our lorries, fell out, put the gear back on the lorries and prepared to go back to Redcar. However, every front door in that street was open and the people came out and said, 'Come in here.' They fed us with sandwiches, buns, cups of tea, anything they could clap their hands on. It was a welcome like nothing on earth.

Each night a soldier's job is to go and have a look at the detail, the orders for the next day. That night, on orders, there was a draft being formed to go out to the CMF (Central Mediterranean Forces) and the MEF (Middle East Forces), and the whole group of us that had got off of the boat several weeks before, were on it! I thought, 'What mobs are now in the Middle East and CMF? It'll be the 2/5th, 2/6th and 2/7th Queens, so I don't want to go back there. No way.' All these Regular soldiers were moaning and swearing, so the sergeant-major came out of the office and said, 'What the hell's going on out here?' Everybody tried to tell him. He said, 'Hold it, hold it. One talk.' One of the blokes said, 'We only got off the bloody boat fourteen days ago. We've just come back from the Far East and Middle East.' So the Sergeant-Major said, 'Who sent you here? This is a Holding Battalion, forming drafts to go overseas. What are you lot doing here?' We didn't know. He went back into the office, got on the phone, and I don't know what he did, but afterwards he said, 'Right, fall out, go back to your bunks, see you in the morning.' The next day they sorted us out. I was sent to Maidstone, the 13th Infantry Training Center (ITC), on Corps training. Here I came into contact with 'National Servicemen', if you would like to call them that. The intakes arrived, did six weeks basic, how to wear a uniform, drill, salute officers, how to wipe your arse, the minor things. Then ten weeks really 'bashing', that is assault courses, the hard part of the training. My routine was 0630 rouse, 0730 breakfast, 0830 muster parade. After that, periods of instruction followed all day on the Bren, mortars and such like (except for NAAFI breaks and meals). Sometimes there was night work, plus of course the usual bullshit and discipline. At the end of the sixteen weeks was pass out parade and seven days leave prior to posting to a battalion. It was all quite interesting, but the British Army would always go to ridiculous lengths. You could go ten weeks without having a bath, but if you had a nicely Blancoed belt with the brasses polished, you were all right.

One day in the Corporal's Mess one of them came over pointing at the tapes on his arm and saying, 'Look at that!' A stripe is made up of little chevrons and normally they had to be Blancoed, but he had indelible blue-pencilled between the chevron, and white-taped the next one. So he had a little blue, little white, little blue, little white, all the way down the chevron and up the other side, instead of just one white streak. It must have taken him hours. Of course everybody went up in the air. 'Get out of it, bullshitter! If the RSM sees that he'll have the lot of us doing it!' Our RSM was the famous Tasker, Queen's Royal Regiment, and for an RSM he was short but a very, very smart man, and by Christ what a voice! He wasn't a bad bloke though. The chevron incident made me decide that I was not going to soldier here much longer, and my prayers were answered shortly after. In September 1943 Colonel Charlie Vaughan, ex-RSM of the Coldstream Guards, now in charge of the Commando Basic Training Centre at Achnacarry, arrived. I had all of our training platoon in the gym to listen to this officer giving a lecture on No. 3 Commando's exploits in North Africa, Sicily and Italy. Finally, he said, 'They need reinforcement. They'll be coming back to England and we need people to go and join them. It's hard but we look after you. The officers are ready to take your name if you want to volunteer.' I decided, 'That's for me,' but by this time everybody in England knew what Commando soldiers were, about the training and what they did, so nobody moved. Who wants to be a Commando when in forty-eight hours you could be dead? Anyway, I marched up, halted, saluted and said, 'Sir, I want to volunteer.' He said, 'I'm told you cannot because you are on permanent staff of this establishment. Training men is an important job.' So I said, 'What do I have to do then, Sir?' 'All you can do is get permission from your Colonel.' I knew that I had to put in a request to the RSM for an interview with the Colonel and that would take forever, but I thought, 'No. Take the bull by the horns.' A pace to the rear, salute, gone. I ran down the hill to the Camp Headquarters and the RSM was there. As soon as I saw him I skidded to a halt. 'Sir.' 'What do you want?' 'I want to see the CO, Sir.' 'Can't see the Colonel, you need to put in a request...' 'Yes Sir, I know, but if I don't do it now, I won't get a chance.' That's why I say that Tasker was all right. He asked me what the problem was, so I told him I wanted to volunteer for Commando service. He understood. He said, 'Wait there,' went into the Colonel's office, came out and said, 'March in.' I went in, saluted and said, 'I know this is unorthodox, Colonel, but if I don't do this now, I'm not going to get another chance.' 'What is it?' he replied. 'I wish to volunteer for the Commandos.' He said, 'Aren't you happy here?' 'Yes Sir, but I want to get in and do a real job.' I heard, 'Request granted, march out,' and was back up that hill like a shot! 'Sir, the Colonel's given me permission.' He said, 'OK. One volunteer,' and another officer took my name. A mate, Don Harding, said, 'You're going? I'm coming too.' Then another bloke, a German Jew, Walter Selby, said, 'I'm coming with you.' Another two decided to come as well. The next thing was to go up to the gym for a medical and an examination unlike anything I had ever encountered. A bloke said, 'Strip off,' and I walked into the first cubicle. The Doctor said, 'Breathe in' and gave me certain exercises to do. Then to the second cubicle. A bloke checked your eyes, the next one your ears, the next one looked at your feet, and if you had flat feet or bunions, you were out. In all there were twelve doctors, each for a different part of the body. When I got to the last one, he said, 'Put your arms up in the air.' Then he put his hands under my armpits and believe it or not, I was sweating, through fear or what I don't know, but he said, 'That's good. Very warm.' When the heat goes from the body the last places to go cold are under the arms and under your private parts. I got dressed and the next thing I knew, I had passed, as had the other four. However, volunteering was not enough. The Commandos chose people because they thought they had potential. You had to volunteer and then be selected.

So there we were, in September 1943, waiting for orders, but instructions soon came to head down to Wrexham in North Wales.

Chapter 5

Commando Training

Wrexham was the location for the Holding Operational Commando (HOC), a place where all those who were not yet Commandos went en route to joining the outfit and for those returning to a unit after being wounded. We were told to report to the barracks of the Royal Welsh Fusiliers across the road, an annex to the camp, as a barrack block had been set aside for the volunteers forming the next draft. I went towards the barrack room, but before I could walk in a bloke said, 'Take your boots off. There are pads to use!' These were felt pads with loops that went around your feet. The reason they had to be worn was that the floor was so highly polished it resembled glass.

Eventually more of the draft arrived. Most were from the Guards, Welsh, Irish, Scots, Coldstream, Grenadiers and the Armoured Division. Being in such prestigious regiments I asked the 'tankers' why they had volunteered for Commandos. Their response was, 'The bullshit! We had tanks where you couldn't swivel the turrets because there was so much bloody paint on them! We had to paint every other nut on the bogies, red and white. After each exercise, the tanks had to be washed down, repainted where scratched, and the rubber pads on tank tracks polished with blacking! And you want to know why we're volunteering for the Commandos!' I made friends with many of these Guards, particularly Norris, Pritchard, Dickinson and MacMillan.

Shortly after their arrival we were on a train to the Highlands, finally reaching a station called Spean Bridge. We went to get onto the platform but the waiting Commando instructors said, 'No. Get out the other side.' This meant jumping down onto the track, crossing it and then getting up onto the platform on the other side.

We had been sitting on that train for ages and all the joints were stiff so I suppose they wanted to see our agility. Then it was, 'Kit bags on the lorry.' Everybody thought, 'Good, we'll get a ride up to the camp.' Wrong. 'Fall in, in threes.' Up to attention, 'Right turn, by the left, quick march!' and as usual for Scotland, it was raining. It turned out to be eight miles to the camp, all of it up and down hill to Achnacarry House, Lord Cameron of Lochiel's abode, which had been taken over by the Army for training purposes. For someone who was pretty fit, and I was because of the corps training, it was not too bad. I had a rifle and was wearing battledress and battle order, which was a haversack on your back containing such things as a ground sheet, mess tins, knife, fork, spoon, dish cloth or spare socks.

Reaching the camp, we marched in and passed a Nissen hut on the right hand side which was the guardroom. In front of it was a line of graves, and everybody thought, 'Bloody hell! Are they real ones?' However, the men who had made the mistakes were in real cemeteries. Each grave was inscribed with 'This man failed to do this ... this man failed to do that ...'

We fell in and an instructor began to explain what was going to happen. At that point three men who had not been able to keep up walked into the camp. They were wearing overcoats and full Service marching order, which was a large pack on your back, haversack on your left-hand side, water bottle on the right, respirator on your chest. He instructed them to wait where they were. He then said to us, 'If you've got any stripes on your arm, take them off, because everybody starts as a Trooper here.' So not only did you volunteer to be selected, you could also drop rank and lose pay.

We were then ordered to fall out and go to our accommodation. The fortunate ones got Nissen huts, the not so fortunate, tents. I was in an eight-man bell tent. The luxury was there were only six of us!

After making ourselves as comfortable as possible we were told to be on parade at 0600 hours the next morning, washed, shaven and weapons as per good state.

The three blokes who had turned up late had been sent to the Orderly Room and given railway warrants, RTU'd for not keeping up. Asking, 'Is there any transport to the station?' they got the reply, 'What are your bloody feet for? Get!' This was our introduction to the Commandos.

The next morning I got up and dressed in training detail: denims and battle order, full water bottle, mess tins, groundsheet, gas cape, rifle and bayonet. I picked up my towel, shaving brush and kit, went out of the tent and of course with Scotland in the winter, it was dark. I said to one of the boys there, 'Where's the ablutions?' 'Straight over there.' So I go 'straight over there' and met another bloke coming back with a towel over his shoulder. 'Where's the ablutions mate?' 'Just over there,' he said. Again, I go 'just over there' and find some blokes kneeling on the ground. 'Where's the ablutions?' They responded, 'Here, in the river!' I said, 'I can't shave in the dark, I can't use my mirror,' to which one of them replied, 'Don't you know where your face is then?' So I was swiftly shaving by feel. After that it became normal routine. You just ran over there with a vest or stripped to the waist and hit the water straight away. It was no good doing it slowly, hit the cold water and wash, get it over and done with.

Breakfast was at 0700 hours. Outside the dining hall, another of the few Nissen huts, was a dustbin that contained something resembling pig's swill. Nobody took much notice of it. We went in with mess tin, knife, fork, spoon. Breakfast was bacon, bread and jam. Afterwards, it was muster parade and then into the training. From morning until night, it was go, go, go. There was no five-minute smoke time or canteen break, you would go right up to lunchtime. Half an hour later it was straight back on parade and away, doing whatever task you were assigned. You could not find a fag and there was no beer. That was it, spartan.

There were three different Troops on the course, each containing about seventy men. We formed Laycock Troop. Training-wise, we did everything: small arms training again, drill, skill at arms, field-craft, the assault course, speed marches where we would sprint for 200 yards and then do the next 200 at Light Infantry pace, rock climbing, abseiling, river crossing, watermanship in boats. Of course, each Troop was 'encouraged' to try and beat the other.[10]

I thought I was pretty fit, but after three days I was knackered. Breakfast was never enough, lunch was never enough. There was your ration and that was it. You learned to eat properly, chewing

[10] We had a bloke called James from the Scots Guards, a drill instructor, and Robertson, a small arms instructor who also took drill sometimes.

slowly and digesting it because gulping it down gave you stomach trouble during the training.

By the fourth morning, you had to get something in your guts and everybody had twigged about the dustbin. It was porridge, *buergoo* as it was known, made from oatmeal, salt and water. This would be eaten before the breakfast itself and digested pretty easily. If you didn't get to the dustbin quickly enough and dip in your mess tin, it would all be gone.

One day our programme included drill parade. The weather was appalling, heavy rain and hail. 'They won't hold drill parade in this. They're joking! We must be doing something else.' Wrong. At the stated time, Drill Sergeant James of the Scots Guards arrived. When he screeched at us his voice seemed to come from everywhere: 'Belt, bayonet, rifle. Out there! Fall in. March on, left, right.' The square was a mud heap and in our damp denims and cap comforter we were taken through foot drill, arms drill, everything. We were at the slope and the order was, 'Present arms from the slope'. Our fingers were frozen around the rifle butts, and they expected us to do it as if it was Pirbright Square on a sunny day. It was horrendous. Talk about sadism. But we did it.

During one of the assault landing exercises, I was designated as the painter man in the bow of the boat. This meant that as the others paddled, on nearing the beach, it was my job to dive out and stick an iron spike and line into the ground to stop the boat being washed back out. As we went in, the banshees started, Bren guns were firing, waterspouts going up, smoke, they were creating mayhem. I was looking at the water, trying to judge when it was shallow enough to jump in. Suddenly, grass and green stuff became visible so I thought 'Now,' and I jumped over the side. With my whole battle order on, plus a rifle and the iron spike in my hand, I went straight down about twenty feet! It was freezing. I looked up to see the boat go overhead. 'Oh my God, I've got to get out.' I don't know how but I must have come up out of there like a cork from a champagne bottle! I dug the spike in and then went up the beach with the others.[11]

[11] Years later I was talking to one of the instructors, a fellow called Arthur Leadbetter and he said, 'I was there when it happened. You were the silly sod were you?!'

We continued on up a hill, with me soaking wet, to some false gun positions built there. These were captured, a protection squad set up while the demolition people went in and blew the guns up with dummy charges which just went bang. The second stage of the exercise was evacuation, so when the signal came to retire, it was all back to the boats. Coming down the hill, the Officer Instructor in front of me jumped from a ledge, at the bottom of which was mud. Just as he was getting up I came over the top and landed on his back, pushing him face-first into the mud! Did I get a cursing! Still, I had a soft landing. I got back to the boat and started to paddle. The Instructor fired a burst across our bow, so I held the oar with one hand and gave him a two-fingered salute with the other! He then fired again and blew the oar out of my hand!

This landing was performed so often that those guns must have been 'blown up' ninety-nine times.

It was then back to the camp, and following a debrief, training carried on.

The big event of the day would be a speed march, seven mile, ten mile or twenty mile. Each had to be done in less than a certain time and on the next occasion you had to try and knock at least a minute off your previous time. Upon returning we would immediately go up the hill to a firing range to do some shooting, carry out ten-minute drill on the square or some other delight.

The lessons just followed on one after another and everybody was timed to do each thing. That's how it went on, week after week.

One particular bloke called Chapman could do anything, but he had no head for heights. During a rock climbing exercise he froze just above me. All the climbing instructors were civilian experts and one of them, Spider Leach, was shouting, 'Move your left hand, move to the left,' but Chapman started to tremble and just couldn't do it. He came off the rock face and went straight down my back, nearly taking me with him. He was very lucky because he hit a shale run and slid down with it, like a miniature avalanche, so that took some of the shock of the fall. The instructor just said, 'Get back up there and do it again.' No 'Hard luck son, can't you do it?' Well, he got up and he did it. Getting to the top was not the only goal though, we then had to abseil down, without any fancy kit. The rope went between your legs then over your shoulder and down you went. It meant rope burns on your legs and hands but you did it.

Another exercise was known as the mad minute, during which we charged up a muddy hill, all the while having to surmount obstacles. On reaching the top there was a tree that had a line from which we had to swing across a gorge. The line was only just long enough and when you got to the end of the swing you had to let go, then carry on running down to the bottom of the hill. If you didn't jump and swung back, the platform could not be reached again, leaving you hanging over the middle of the gorge, and there was only one way to go, into the water below. Chapman, poor sod, went across, didn't jump, could not get back and was left hanging. He looked at the instructor and said, 'What am I going to do?' The answer was, 'Let go of the rope!'

The gorge also had to be crossed by monkey crawling along a rope. The knack was to pull your leg up over the rope and slide down it while maintaining your balance. Below, the river was in flood and included lumps of ice. Chapman was on the rope next to me and moved down it a short way, just enough to be over the river, when his legs came off the rope. He said, 'What am I going to do?' I said, 'Don't hang about, get the regain in,' which meant getting his legs back over the rope, but he couldn't. In the end he had to let go and went straight into the drink. Instead of going along with the stream towards scramble nets hanging further down, he kept trying to get up and fight the current, but was knocked over every time. In the end it took two instructors to go in and get him out.

There was also the 'Death Slide', which was a line that crossed the river, the high end being set up in a big tree. You had to throw a toggle rope over it and slide down. As you did so, charges exploded in the water, soaking you again! After one attempt when we had all reached the other side successfully, our chief instructor started to cross when his toggle rope stuck on the line. The only way to get over this was to bounce on the line until you moved again. He bounced, went down a couple of feet and stuck again. Bounced, stuck again. On the next bounce the line broke, sending him straight down into the river to the accompaniment of our cheers! He was all right because downstream, scrambling nets had been positioned on a footbridge. When he got back he said, 'Right. We'll ALL have a laugh tonight.' We had extra drill.

After eleven weeks of such training, we were told that it was the final seven days and a sort of competition week. Everything we did would be the normal training but with even shorter time limits on each task. Usually, for a seven-mile speed march they gave you over an hour to do it, but for this week it was fifty-five minutes, meaning that you had to go a bloody sight faster! Just to make it happy for you, after finishing that, there was a five-miler around the perimeter of the camp that had to be completed in forty-five minutes. You couldn't moan because they might say, 'Right, fifteen mile speed march!' After that it was off up to the range. It just never stopped.

In that last week we also had to do what they called a 'Me and my pal' course. One had a rifle and bayonet, the other a Thompson sub-machine carbine, and you went round a course that finished up by covering each other as you advanced; one moved, one fired, the other moved, the other fired. You did not move unless the other was covering you. At the end of it was a mock-up of an enemy machine gun position. The idea was to say to your mate, 'Grenade.' He pulled the pin out, chucked it, one, two, three, four, UP, IN! Chapman came round, pulled a '36' grenade, a deadly thing, out of his pouch (because unlike the Yanks in the pictures, you didn't have them hanging from your webbing), pulled the pin out, chucked it and immediately jumped in! The bloody grenade exploded and he didn't even get a scratch! Chapman was RTU'd.

When it finally came around to who had passed and failed, only seventeen succeeded from the seventy-five or so men. Consequently, the wastage, RTU'd through ineptitude, injury or on request, was about fifty-eight in total. You needed to have good mates to get through it and I had Norris, Pritchard and Dickinson. No one was an expert at everything, and when one of us was struggling with a specific part of the training the others helped. On one run I had been so exhausted that they had carried me between them, two at a time, until I recovered.

I know every Commando will say this, but I reckon it was the best bloody Troop that went through Achnacarry, because it was winter, and boy, winter in Scotland, what a shock. At Achnacarry it rains every five minutes for half-an-hour! We were wet from start to finish.

There was a parade where we received our green berets. At last, after all of the changing between regiments I was a fully trained nineteen year old soldier, a green-bereted Commando. No words can describe my elation.

The following day, as we were sitting in trucks, waiting to leave Achnacarry for the station, thank Christ, the Royal Marine Engineers had got people up there to put hards down on which to build Nissen huts. Right opposite us a cement mixer was going when suddenly there was a horrific scream. One of the engineers had somehow got his arm tangled up with the cement mixer.

Chapter 6

Commando Life and Preparing for D-Day

The train pulled into Worthing Station in Sussex. NCOs of No. 3 Commando were waiting for us and we were taken to a big private house that had been requisitioned for use as the HQ of the Commando. Next it was upstairs for an interview with the Commanding Officer, Lieutenant Colonel Peter Young, DSO and bar, MC and bar. He had been on the Vaagso, Lofoten and Dieppe raids, served in the North African campaign and had taken part in the attacks on the Agnone gun battery and Ponti dei Malati bridge in Sicily, and the Bova Marina in Italy. He was highly respected. I was with Don Harding, who went into the office first. Then it was my turn. Lieutenant Colonel Young said to me, 'Welcome to 3 Commando.' For a snotty nosed kid, what progress! He gave a brief about the unit and then asked, 'Which Troop would you like to join?' 'Troop, Sir?' 'Let me explain, 1 Troop is an Assault Troop, 2 Troop is heavy weapons, the mortars, number 3 is going to be the Parachute Troop, numbers 4, 5 and 6 are also Assault Troops.' Don was parachute trained, so I guessed he would pick the Parachute Troop, and so I chose 3 Troop. The Colonel confirmed that I was volunteering for parachute duties and I marched outside. Don said, 'I'm going to 4 Troop!' I said, 'You bloody idiot why didn't you go to 3 Troop?' 'Because I've done all of that before.'

So I was in 3 Troop, a volunteer Troop amongst volunteers. It had some bloody good boys: the officers, Captain Roy Westley, Lieutenants Ponsford and Lewis, TSM Coker, Sergeants Dowling, Edwards, Edmunds, Salisbury and Hughes, Corporals Jimmy Synnott and

'Tucker' Jennings. Then Dickinson, Jenkins, MacMillan, Hutt, Good, Ellis Norris, 'Flash' Freeman, 'Ossie' Osbourne, Paddy Harnett, Ted Pritchard, 'Dixie' Dean, Big Bill Garrett, Jackie Barnes, Johnny Abbott, Les Hill and Ted Gowers, to name a few.

Commandos were not sited in barracks, they lived in civilian billets and received an allowance of 6/8 a day for such lodgings and food, which many people thought was danger money. In all, alongside our normal Army pay I was getting about five pounds a week. You also got a ration card every week. At Worthing each Troop was very handily situated in houses around a pub called the Ham Hotel. I was with a bloke called Fred Rabbetts of the East Surrey's. We were told to go to a Mrs Ford at a house named 'Thirsk' (from where we later found, she originated), 168 Lyndhurst Road, right on the corner of a crossroads, opposite the pub. When we arrived nobody was in, and so we stood there with all our kit until the very homely figure of Mrs Ford appeared. 'Hello lads.' 'Ma'am, we've been billeted on you.' She said, 'Yes, I've been waiting for you. Sorry to keep you waiting. Come in and I'll do some eggs and bacon. We'll have a meal later.' We thought, 'This is all right!' She showed us to a big front bedroom, the only thing wrong being the solitary double bed! My immediate thought was, 'The only bloke I sleep with is my brother!' I was used to that at Tottenham, but with no other possible solution we agreed to give it a try.

For that first night the entire Troop had agreed to meet in the Ham Hotel. As we walked in, so the civilians began to walk out, which we thought was highly indelicate of them, but we took no notice, had a drink, returned home and went to bed. Fred, who liked his Black and Tan beer, got up during the night and opened the door of the big wardrobe. I said, 'Oi, what are you doing?' He said, 'I thought it was the loo.' 'No. Out the door, turn left.'

The next day, we reported to our Troops, got on with what we had to do and finally came back to the billet. That evening, it was back over to the Ham Hotel and again, as we entered, the people got up to leave. This time Ted Pritchard and Ellis Norris stood across the door and said, 'What's all this about? Why are you walking out? We're billeted on you, so what are you doing?' An older man said, 'We've heard about you boys. You're all bloody trouble!' 'Trouble? We don't make any trouble. Who are we going to make trouble with?' Anyway, they stayed and we finished up playing dominoes and darts with them. To top the bill, we had a lot of Welsh Guardsmen and at the end of the evening, having downed a few beers, one of them started singing to himself. Then the other boys joined in, so within two days of arrival we had our own Welsh male voice choir entertaining the locals! From that point on, every time we went in there it was, 'Come on, give us a song!'

Unfortunately, that night it was the same sort of caper with Fred Rabbetts, only this time he opened the bloody window and peed into the front garden! The third night was the end. He came in late and I was already in bed, half a sleep. He got in the bed and suddenly I thought, 'What the hell ...?' He was groping me! I gave him an elbow, bounced him out the bed and said, 'What's your game?' He said, 'I'm sorry. It must be the bloody drink. I thought you were my wife!' In the morning I told Mrs Ford what had happened. She was not going to stand for that and so got him transferred, although we still remained friends.

*　*　*

Before our first leave we were warned about getting into in any trouble. If the police became involved it meant immediate RTU. Use of close combat skills was expressly forbidden.

I arrived home to find that my father was still away in the Army, now with 919 Heavy Transport Company RASC. The next day I was passing the local pub, The Railway Tavern. With my green beret on, feeling as proud as punch I went in for a pint. After a while, who should come in but my father, home on leave. He took one look at me and said, 'You silly bastard, what have you done? Commandos!' Their reputation was such that everybody thought that once in action they only had forty-eight hours to live. I said, 'Dad. At least I know I've joined the best.' We stood in the saloon bar talking about things when in came a bloke called Tommy Weston, an old school bully and a nasty piece of work. Recognizing me, he passed by saying, 'I thought they only took men in the Commandos.' I just ignored him. However, he then stood directly behind me and continued to make sarcastic remarks. I carried on talking, but gradually my father began to look at me in a strange way and I knew that something had to be done. We were beside the bar and I glanced back to ascertain Weston's position. From the way I was standing he would expect me to turn to my right to face him, so I moved to the left. As he turned around I brought my right fist around and connected with his face. He slid along the bar and collapsed flat on his back. I turned back to my father who said, 'I'm glad you did that because if you hadn't, I would have!'

* * *

Upon our return to Worthing, training started straight away for what we knew would be the invasion of Europe. We went up to Scotland, to Oban and Salen in the Hebrides, for seamanship training on different types of craft, initiations to the Landing Craft Infantry Small (LCI(s)), Landing Craft Assault (LCA) etc. We were based on HMS *Prince Albert* from Tormentor, Pompey, the shore base for Royal Navy Landing Craft crews. The ship was an ex-Dover to Ostend ferry, pressed into service with the Royal Navy and known as 'Lucky Albert' because she had survived many bombing attempts.

Then it was back to Warsash on the south coast to meet our matelot crews. We started Section and Troop training and I became a Section Bren Gunner again. The reasons for having to do the various parts of the training were always explained to us, it was not just a case of 'Do it because I say so.' The exercises were done all over the South Downs to Arundel: river crossings, beach landings, wet and dry, mostly wet, range work, live firing exercises, but with nearly always the same objective – capture Arundel Castle. We would go to Portsmouth, board a landing craft, travel to somewhere east of Littlehampton, begin landing and then run to Arundel. If no landing craft were available we would run from Worthing. Either way, on approaching Arundel the first thing that had to be done was to capture the railway bridge and station. Then it was move on to the River Arun which was tidal, so it might be in, might be out, but again, either way we had to cross it. There was no going across the bridge. Sometimes collapsible boats were used, other times just a rope. Once across, the last task was to scale the walls of the castle and this was done either by forming a human pyramid or by grappling irons. Afterwards, the Troop Commander might say, 'There are lorries round the corner to take you back to Worthing,' but you would get round there, not see anything and think, 'He must mean the next corner!' You would find them all right, in Worthing itself! They called it a 'Gutser'. On the occasions when they did actually have transport waiting, it was only to get you back for some other bloody reason. Everybody would be lined up outside the Troop Headquarters and be told, 'That's it, training is finished for today.' Then out would come the Troop Commander and say, 'Number 1, A and B Sections. Exercise tonight, starting at ...,' and that was you done. It was never any good saying to a girl, 'I'll see you tomorrow night,' because you never knew what was going to happen.

I went on a specialist course for mines and demolitions at Lewes and it was very enjoyable laying booby traps and blowing things up. There was an exercise where we were taken to inspect a bridge on the Shoreham to Worthing road. Every bridge was built with a space underneath for the location of explosives to destroy it. Back at HQ the officer in charge of the course said, 'I want you to write a report laying down what you need to blow that bridge. I want it damaged in such a way as to stop traffic using it. Take into account that you are going to be dropped by parachute.' We all decided what was required to do the job, how you were going to blow it, where to put the charges and things like that. Just destroying the centre section is no good because the buttresses are still available to be worked on, but if it is blown at the end, the buttress is destroyed and the whole thing drops. I chose this orthodox way, using what I thought was the normal amount of explosive which was safe to handle on the move. When the officer received these reports, he read them and one in particular caught his attention. He said, 'I must read you this gentlemen. This man is going to parachute in carrying 500 pounds of explosive! Would that student mind standing up.' He got such a cheer. Somebody at the back said, 'Who's going to dig you out?!' If it had been me I wouldn't have stood up!

Each day we would go onto the Downs to blow things up, carry out cratering, cut railway lines and so forth. Before returning to the camp the unused stores were laid out and the officer would say, 'Load the lorry,' and every night someone would pick something up and it would go BANG! There were five anti-lifting devices available, like release or pull switches, and these booby-traps caught nearly everyone out. My turn involved a dummy German Teller mine; when, after having made a quick check, I lifted it, BANG!

I did several things on the course that I should not have done, one of them while cratering a road. For this, a tube was banged into the ground, and a couple of gun cotton primers inserted that had electric detonators on the end of a line which was pulled. The small explosion made a chamber, leaving a tube and a chamber. The wires were brought out through the tube and Amatol poured in, a yellow powdery explosive, until the chamber was half full. Then another set of primers and detonators was put down, the rest of the chamber filled and the tube taken out. The last man back carried the wires and connected them to the dynamo. 'Ready to go ... 3, 2, 1, BOOM,' a big crater in the road. However, on this occasion we could also hear the whirring noise of something flying through the air. It was the bloody tube! I had forgotten to remove it.

At the end of the last day on the Downs, we got the usual order, 'Put the stores back on the wagon.' Nothing happened. No booby-traps. The officer was talking to somebody, so I said, 'Give me one of those release switches.' I primed it, put it in the passenger door of the lorry and shut the door. We were all sitting in the back, the tailboard was up and he came round and said, 'Righto lads, back we go. It's the end of the course.' He went to open the door and BANG! We all fell about laughing! He just said, 'What smart Alec did that?' It just goes to show, you should never get too confident!

* * *

Towards the end of April the Troop was supplied with fold-up parachute bicycles. They were OK, but didn't have any brakes! Also, when folded they were very unwieldy, horrible to carry. Two butterfly nuts in the middle of the frame locked it and you made sure they were as tight as possible, but this was not as easy as it seemed. During an exercise over the Downs at Rottingdean, I was cycling down a track and went to turn when the thing folded up on me. I finished up in a ditch. Several pile-ups occurred while going down hills. It was comical, a big heap of bikes and bodies, but nobody was injured. We rode all over Sussex and Hampshire. The bikes were not supposed to be used except on duty or during exercises, but people used to go into town on them. If you had a bike, why pay for a bus? They were a pretty handy thing. One night on telephone watch at Headquarters, I was informed of a sick officer on the other side of Broadwater Green. I walked up the road, banged on the door of our Doctor, Ned Moore and explained. He said, 'Right, I'll go and see him. Have you got transport?' I said, 'Yes, a Para bike.' He got on it and rode off!

During another exercise on the Downs, with the Rifle Brigade as opposition, the bike again folded up on me. By the time I had got everything going again, the rest of the Troop had disappeared. So I cycled down the road when suddenly a Lloyd Carrier, a general purpose tracked vehicle for carrying mortars, machine guns, ammunition appeared. It was the enemy. I dismounted behind a hedge and crept forward. With the Bren gun slung and a loaded Colt 45 in my hand, I continued to creep forward until I was right up to the men in the Carrier. Then I said, 'Hands up. You're my prisoners!' Being Rifle Brigade people, they turned round, looked at me and laughed! Again I said, 'You are my prisoners.' One of them said, 'Hold on. There are five of us and only one of you, and we've got a Carrier,' so I said, 'I've got a Colt 45 here and if you don't put your bloody hands up, I'll use it!' 'Yeah, get out of it.' I pointed the gun in the air and fired two rounds. Amazingly, they cut two telephone wires! With the parting comment, 'You're mad!', they got in the Carrier and shot away. There was not much else I could do. I put the pistol back in the holster, got on the bike and peddled down the road. Approaching a junction I could again hear tracks, so this time I got up onto a bank, took the Bren gun off the sling, and yet another Carrier stopped. There was an officer in it and a big map, amongst other things. I stood up on the bank and said, 'Right. You are prisoners!' The Bren gun pointing at them had a magazine containing twenty-eight rounds. Talk about take the exercise seriously. The Rupert said, 'Oh my Gawd! I can't be a prisoner, I'm running the exercise!' So I said, 'All right then, I haven't seen you, and you haven't seen me' and we parted company.

Continuing on the road to Brighton, a 15 cwt truck came along, so I stopped it. Lo and behold it belonged to the Rifle Brigade. The driver said, 'What do you want mate?' I said, 'I'm trying to get back to Headquarters.' He invited me to jump on the back, which I did, holding the bike over the tailboard. He drove me to Headquarters all right, HIS headquarters. I wandered about a bit, came round a corner and there was a queue of Rifle Brigade soldiers. I asked one of them what was going on. He said, 'We're getting a bit of grub.' I therefore put the bike and the Bren gun against the wall, got the mess tins and utensils out of my pack, and lined up with them. I went past the cook, got my meal and a cup of tea and sat down amongst them on the wall, eating my grub. One said, 'You're well kitted out,' because I was wearing a Para smock (my green beret was stashed). I replied, 'Yeah, it's new camouflage kit. Actually, I'm a runner.' The food was good, so I had another bowl and found myself amongst a group who were discussing what they were going to do that night. They had found out that the Commandos had parked their transport (transport . . . that's a laugh! It was a couple of jeeps and trailers) in a big barn and the Rifle Brigade was going to send a patrol out to see what they could do about it. I got back on the bike and rode away, eventually finding 3 Commando lines. When I reached the Troop, I found the RSM and said, 'I want to speak to the Colonel, Sir.' 'What's it about?' 'I've got some information.' He took me to Peter Young, or Bungy as we now fondly knew him, who said, 'What is it?' 'I've got some information Sir, that might be of interest. The Rifle Brigade is planning to mount a raiding patrol into our MT lines tonight.' 'What time is this happening?' 'I don't know the time but they are going to wait until it's dark.' He said, 'Thank you very much.'

That night, the MT lines did everything as normal. When the RB lads came up, as soon as they got into the barn, the doors were shut behind them. A reception committee came out of the rafters and wallop! That was good!

At the end of that exercise all of our firepower was assembled on the cliffs at Rottingdean and at the given signal, opened up. There were Vickers, Bren guns, mortars, just firing out to sea to get rid of ammunition. The terrible cacophony must have put the fear of Christ up a lot of local people.

Following that, we were to start parachute training. Normally, volunteers to join the Parachute Regiment went to Hardwick Hall for basic training and if they passed that, moved on to the Parachute Training School at Ringway to do the jumps. However, Commandos were deemed fit enough already and so went straight to the jump training. 3 Troop's training was unique in as much as they brought the parachute training gear down to Worthing, instead of us going up to Ringway. During this I had the privilege of knocking the PTI over! We were on the swing, all kitted out and he said, 'When you get the order, "GO" …,' which was normally on a forward swing, '… release yourself, land and roll.' He might say, 'Forward left, GO' or 'Forward, right, GO.' Anyway, I was coming forward and he said, 'GO!', but the silly sod was standing in the way, so I landed on him! No damage was done, so I don't know why he got so mad, it was his fault not mine. However, as a Troop, No. 3 did not complete the course, that is the jumps from aircraft, because Lieutenant Colonel Young stated that there was no time slot available. We had to wait.[12]

Later we found out that not only had we volunteered for parachute duties, we were also available to land by submarine if needed, and that meant an extra lot of training. All we did though was visit a submarine at the Royal Navy base in Gosport to see what it was like. We never actually got around to doing anything with a submarine.

*   *   *

The training routine next took us to Limehouse in East London, behind Brick Lane. The area was devastated, rows of normal terraced houses bombed to pieces. The exercises, mostly breaking, entering and house-to-house street fighting, were carried out using live ammunition. We were trying out different techniques, 'mouse-holing' from one house to another, blowing holes through the walls, although with this type of house we found there was no need to use a charge. A burst with a Bren gun of about half a magazine would make the necessary weakness and by just kicking the wall, a hole would appear. Upstairs, the same thing had to be done while those on the rooftops could just gallop along. Consequently, the blokes on the roof would get to the end of the terrace before those inside and therefore quicker than the retreating enemy and so catch them as they came out.

About a week was spent in this area, living and sleeping as per front line conditions, so we were in a nice state. The biggest incident turned out to be when the powers that be contrived to change 'Flash' Freeman's 2-inch mortar for a new type with a longer barrel, giving it more range. While using it to lay a smokescreen down for the lads

[12] My Parachute Association number is 18410 and the instructors were Major Beaumont, Captain Black, Fox and Sugden.

to cross an open space, he put the bomb in the barrel, judged the angle, pulled the lanyard and away it went. The bomb sailed up and over the perimeter, a railway embankment, into a ship's chandler's shop in Cable Street which immediately caught fire. Everybody in there thought that it came from the sky. Well it did, but from us! So we were called across to help. We saved as much of the equipment as possible, but eventually had to stop because the paint on the upstairs metal windows was melting and one of the men got some down the back of his neck, causing a nasty burn. We left the Fire Brigade to take over and went back to the bombed area minus one of our blokes, Harry Ward, who had a look around, found the owner's sugar and tea and brought it back with him. So we had a brew-up on the owner.

At the end of this training, one of the officers said, 'Do any of you boys come from London? If so, take a lorry and go home for a couple of hours. Clean up and rejoin at Worthing.' Charing Cross was made the RV point and on the way, I found that the driver lived at the top end of St Anne's Road, Wood Green. I lived near the other end of St Anne's Road, and asked if he could drop me there, which he did. I got off the lorry with a Bren gun, ammunition, all my kit, looking a right state. I arrived home and gave the old lady quite a shock. After a quick clean up and something to eat I went back down Grove Road to the junction with St Anne's Road and bumped into my sister Gloria. I hated sentimental goodbyes and had never had anybody come to the station. She started to walk along the road with me. I looked up and saw the lorry coming down the road so I said, 'Gloria, do me a favour, I haven't got any matches. Run home and get me a box.' Off she went, the lorry pulled up and I was away. I just couldn't take that sort of thing.

*   *   *

On occasions, being a Commando attracted unwanted attention. For instance, Don Harding and I were having a quiet pint with some Frenchmen of No. 10 Commando in the Cranbourne Arms behind Leicester Square Station. In came a party of Yanks with a woman, possibly of ill repute. After a few drinks they started telling the woman to strip off. She refused. They insisted, so Don told them to leave her alone. The Yanks looked at us, two British soldiers (by this time the French lads had gone). Five onto two, not bad odds. So the first Yank threw a right-hand punch at Don who parried the blow and countered with a right, straight to the gut. Then all hell broke out and we began to enjoy ourselves. Fists, elbows, heads. Meanwhile, the woman remembered the French wearing green berets like ours, so she ran out and brought them back. No contest. Five very battered Yanks. The landlord said, 'Right lads, scarper before the MPs get here,' and the woman made a quick getaway too.

Another time, we held a dance in the Worthing Municipal Hall, opposite the cinema and all the lads were there with their girl-friends. Then three lorries full of Canadians pulled up outside and realizing there was a party going on, decided to gatecrash. We all got the message 'Out.' We walked out, left the women there and let the Canadians take over. Outside, Jimmy Synnott ordered us to go back to our billets and get our entrenching tool handles, which we duly did. The plan was to go back in, form a ring around the dance floor and slowly walk towards the centre. However, before entering, Synnott said to myself and Ted Pritchard, 'Stand at the top of the stairs,' as there were about four steps down to the foyer, 'and as they come out, help them down!' The boys went in and began to close the circle, pushing the dancers towards the middle of the floor and with the women ducking, running and screaming, some of the Canadians started throwing punches. They were then given what they had asked for, and as the Canucks came towards the doors, we helped them on their way with a big whack from the entrenching tool. Outside the entrance were the Canadian Provo, British Military Police and the local police, but they never came in and afterwards said, 'Why should we come in when you're doing the job for us?!' The Canadians were bundled back onto the lorries and driven away.

The following morning, everybody was summoned to the local cinema. In walked Colonel Young and everybody stood to attention. He got up onto the stage and we all sat down. There was not a sound, no coughing, nothing. He then proceeded to give everybody a right rollicking and finished up with words that we never forgot. 'I am not having any of my Commando soldiers getting involved in public brawls. If I find any of you fighting, I'll have you RTU'd. But on the other hand, if I find any man running away from a good fight, I'll RTU you!' So that was that. But it was a good fight!

*   *   *

The landing training became a grind, Worthing, Littlehampton, run to Arundel, capture the railway station, cross the river ... Some evenings were spent pleasantly in the Ham Hotel, that is of course when there were no night exercises.

During May the Troop did some training at Findon, on the golf links of all places, practising fire and movement. By now, this had been hammered into us and was just another one of those things. My gun was in position in a sand bunker. An umpire officer with a posh accent said, 'You can't move, you're under fire, pinned down.' So that was it, I couldn't move. What he forgot was that I had a Section Leader and when he said, 'Prepare to move,' you moved, it didn't matter what was happening, you moved. That's exactly what happened. The order came, 'Section, prepare to move with me.' So I was up with the gun, moving, and this Rupert said, 'You're under fire, you're pinned down, you're dead!' What did I do? Played the silly sod. I threw the Bren up in the air, grabbed my chest, screamed 'Aaaahhhh', and began writhing on the ground, just like in the cinema. The gun came down barrel first into the ground.[13]

I was put on a charge for playing about and the following morning was up in front of the Troop Commander, Captain Westley, who said, 'You are not a responsible person, and being a Bren gunner is a responsible position. I am taking the gun away from you and giving it to Parker.' So I surrendered the Bren and returned to being a rifleman.

* * *

At the end of May, we packed our kit and prepared to move to a concentration area. As we were leaving, Mrs Ford, bless her heart, brought out two quart flagons of brown ale. 'Take that with you, you're bound to need a drink!'

The concentration area, at Titchfield Park near Warsash, was run and staffed by our American friends. Here, we were under canvas. There was plenty of dust and of course US of A food. Instead of using a set of mess tins, our food was dished out on Yankee trays that had different compartments for each thing. When served, they

[13] Of course the flash eliminator was full of mud, but it didn't mean that the gun was inoperative because I'd got a spare barrel.

all slopped over into each other so you had a mixture of meat, vegetables and pudding.

One of the Yanks had a lament, the words of which were something like, 'I joined the goddamned American Army. I travelled 3,000 miles across the United States of America, I travelled 3,000 miles across the Atlantic Ocean to a place called England. I'm watching a load of Limey lads train and get ready to go to battle. And what am I doing? I'm shovelling and burning shit!' He was a lavatory attendant!

In the evenings there was nothing to do, although there was a cinema. We watched a film called *Claudia*, and they must have put it on every night to make us yearn to get out of the camp.

We went out on a short march, perhaps two miles, and by now we were so primed for action that it was like taking a greyhound for a ten-yard run. No contact with civilians was permitted, but whether we were on the back of a lorry or marching, if there were any bits of skirt going by, it was always wolf whistles and banter. It happens!

Briefing sessions started for D-Day. The first one was given using aerial photos laid out as a map. A town could be seen, the coast, and a canal and river going inland, but it was impossible to tell the location. It was just a part of the French coast. The whole of the 1st Special Service Brigade comprising 3, 4 and 6 Commandos plus 45 Royal Marine Commando, was landing on a beach codenamed 'Sword'. We were told, 'You will be landing on a section of the beach codenamed Queen Red, but won't be landing first because the poor bastards in the infantry got that, the East Yorks ..., 3 Troop, you will get to the bridges across the canal and river. You will not stop for anything. Bypass any opposition. 3 Troop, you will get to the bridges ..., you will get to the bridges.' In the end we went to bed dreaming 'You will get to the bridges.'

To help us on what was about a five-mile journey inland to the bridges, we had the fold-up bikes. If the bridges had been blown when we got there, our crossing was to be made using dinghies that were to be parachuted in. Once across both bridges, the whole Commando was to head north along the coast for the village of Cabourg.

Ammunition was issued, '36' fragmentation, '69' stun, and smoke grenades, also three 3-inch mortar bombs per man strapped onto the handlebars; an extra 30 lb to carry besides our kit and weapons.

Then finally it happened. We left the camp and embarked at Warsash, right in front of a pub. 3 Commando boarded LCI(S) numbers 501, 509, 512, 535 and 538. 3 Troop, on LCI 501, stacked the bicycles and got below. In the early evening everybody cast off. As we moved out to sea, it was quite choppy so I opted to spend the journey in the starboard 20 mm Oerlikon gun position, smoking and talking with the matelots.

Chapter 7

D-Day

It is early morning and there are a lot of ships about, ours in line astern, but nothing is happening. It could be just another exercise. I go below to have some breakfast. There was no cookhouse on an LCI(S), so I got hold of a can of self-heating soup. I tried and tried again to light the fuse that ran through the middle but it just kept spluttering and going out, so that idea was ditched. There was a short ladder up to the deck, and poking my head through the hatch I could see that all the boats had moved to line abreast. Just as I got my feet on the deck there was one almighty bang. 'What was that? By Christ, it's the coast!' All flaming hell then let loose with shells, machine guns, smoke and fires. There was a sudden enormous bang on our port side and a destroyer just broke in two and went down.[14]

On the run-in to the beach the matelots came up ready to put the ramps out and help us off. I suddenly realized that bullets were flying about. With a couple of hundred yards to go, on our starboard side I saw LCI(S) 509, carrying 6 Troop, take a hit from a shell, straight on the nose. The craft kept going forward and people were jumping off as she slowly began to go under. We picked up our bikes and prepared to land. The ramps were pushed out over rollers, their only connection to the boat being a couple of rope lines. One ramp was hit almost immediately, leaving us with a solitary ramp to use. The first bloke off was Johnny Dowling, the second, MacMillan, about six-foot-four, and me, number three, all lugging bikes. The ramps were not very wide. How you were supposed to

[14] This was the Norwegian destroyer, *Svenner*, which was torpedoed by German E-Boats.

keep your balance I don't know, especially with the tide, but you had to concentrate a hundred percent in trying to get everything right and quickly. You know what you have got to do and just do it. We went down the ramp, hit the beach and there was an immediate explosion. I was blown to the left, flat on my back. Johnny Dowling got knocked up the beach, MacMillan went back into the sea. Dowling was picked up by two German prisoners and taken back to the boat. MacMillan got fished out of the sea by a matelot with a gaff. Somebody stepped over me and said, 'Get up Scotty, you ain't hurt,' so I picked up the bike and carried on. People were going down and you were just following the mob. There was no one to say, 'This is No. 2 Section, this is No. 3 Section,' we were all mixed up. Halfway up the beach we stopped again and I thought, 'If we stay here, I'm going to dig a bleedin' hole and get out of it!' Anyway someone said, 'Let's get going' and we continued up the beach, crossed a road with tramlines, straight into an area that the Germans had flooded. There was no cover. We struggled on through mud, reeds and water, sometimes knee deep, sometimes up to our armpits. A few of the shorter blokes had it up to their chins. All the time the enemy was lobbing mortar bombs at us, but in the mud they just went PLOP. We could hear machine gun fire and there were blokes going down left and right, but if you were not hit, you didn't worry. Johnnie Johnson was hit and whatever it was took half his bloody ear off. He just went 'Aahh.' All blood. I stopped to have a word with him and he said, 'See you Scotty' and went back to the beach. A Nebelwerfer opened fire on the beach and made us glad we were no longer there. We carried on and came to the Colleville–Hermanville road. The first thing we did was pull out all the reeds and mud from the chain, then mounted up and rode away to our first objective, the canal bridge. We went down the road like the Tour de France! Other mobs were seen on the way, but from Colleville, through St Aubin D'Arquenay right down to Le Port, the northern part of Benouville, it was quiet. 3 Troop was the leading Troop of the 1st Special Service Brigade. Opposite the Church in Le Port, a lone Para was sitting with a shattered leg up on a chair, guarding a little knot of prisoners. He looked at us and said, 'Where the f*** have you been?' The usual British greeting, 'Bollocks!' was my reply as I went past and on towards Benouville Town Hall.

We turned left at the Town Hall, and down the slope we could see the bridge. On the left hand side of the road was a garden with a little bank, and we got down beside it. This was fine if fire was coming from the left, but it was coming from the right. We were about seventy-five yards from the bridge and it was like a beehive. There were rounds hitting it from all sides, mostly appearing to come from a large building down the canal on the right, the Maternity Home in the Chateau de Benouville.[15] On the other side of the bridge a gun in an emplacement was trying to hit them, WHOOMPF! The Airborne were also using a German tracked vehicle with an ack-ack gun. Somehow five of us, myself, Campbell, Jimmy Synnott, Ossie Osbourne and one other had got in front of the rest of the Troop, and just as we realized the bank was not doing us any good, someone said, 'Get on your bikes, you'll probably get away with it!' Well, we were soldiers and there to do a job, so we all jumped on our bikes and pedalled like mad across the bridge. Campbell was the unlucky one. He was shot straight through the neck and went down in one big heap with the bike right in front of me and I was lucky not to collide with him.[16] Reaching the other side of the bridge, I saw a smouldering German vehicle and thought, 'That's solid; that's protection' and got behind that. Jimmy Synnott and the others went into a ditch on the left hand side. I suddenly realized that there was a strong smell of roasting pork, looked in and saw three incinerated occupants.

I was called to join the others in the ditch and shortly after, the rest of 3 Troop came up. We then crossed the River Orne bridge and halted just beyond it. The Brigade now came under the command of the 6th Airborne Division, and due to German attacks east of the Orne, the majority of 3 Commando was to be diverted to Ranville. However, Captain Westley and Lieutenant Ponsford received orders from Lord Lovat for 3 Troop to help the 9th Parachute Battalion which was in difficulty in the village of Amfreville on the Breville Ridge.

[15] Bill Bailey (2nd Ox and Bucks) was standing by the bridge, near the gun. Wally Parr was working the gun in the pit, trying to hit the water tower/maternity home area. We met again on the same spot in 1984.

[16] The film *The Longest day* was totally wrong regarding Lovat and Bill Millin, his piper, being the first commandos to reach the bridge. Campbell was shot long before Lovat got there. Also, Lovat was NOT wearing a white sweater!

We began walking up the road leading to Ranville. While doing so, a sergeant of the 7th Parachute Battalion was hit by something which ignited a phosphorous grenade in his pocket. He was burning up and an officer walked out and shot him. It was all that could be done for him.

The road forked left and right. We went left and there was a small row of houses with front gardens. Two German motorbikes lay in the hedge and one of the lads said, 'I'm going to have one of these,' but I warned him off because they looked suspicious. I took a closer look and they were indeed booby-trapped.

We continued on our bikes along the Sallenelles road. It was like a Sunday afternoon ride. Reaching the Ecarde crossroads, just below Amfreville, Captain Westley said, 'This is it.' We turned in, dumped our bikes and mortar bombs, which turned out to be useless as somehow the charges had been removed, formed up in our Sections and went up the hill. I had a loaded rifle with bayonet fixed and a grenade handy. I felt very determined and was saying to myself, 'I don't know what I'm going to meet but if it's wearing field grey, he's going to cop it.' The advance was the usual procedure. The leading Section went so far, got down, then the next one passed on, leap-frogging each other. Nearing the top of the slope, everyone was all eyes and ears. We approached a wall where the road veered slightly to the right. On the left was the gable end of a house and in the apex was a little window. Everybody must have been watching that window when the muzzle end of a rifle appeared, a badly trained infantryman. I don't know how many people fired but the window just disappeared with the strikes and the rifle fell out. We didn't know whether the bloke had been hit or not. As we came around the bend a Russian Maxim machine gun opened up. Ossie Osbourne and Tucker Jennings immediately returned fire, but Westley was hit in the wrist and elbow, Paddy Harnett through the arse, 'Dixie' Dean in the guts and Abbott had his leg cut off. We moved back a short distance down the hill. The soldier firing this Maxim must have been a bit nervous because if he had waited for fifteen seconds he would have had two Sections of 3 Troop in the open and without hope of taking cover. Ossie then went forward to get Dixie Dean who was lying out in the open with Jerry still trying to hit him. He was a big bloke, Dixie, and it was not all nicey, nicey, like in the pictures. Ossie grabbed him by the webbing, dragged him back and

Mum and Dad

At Lancasterian School,
aged about 13

School leaving card

'nore rusty, stinking bucket you could not wish to find' – the SS *Koscuisko*

London Branch of the Commando Veterans Association with members of 59 Commando and a couple
Para friends! *(Dick Goodwin)*

With Dad while in the Queen's, early 1942

Member of 3 Commando

My friend Walter Selby, Lt Col Peter 'Bungy' Young, the CO of No 3 Commando, and the Doctor, Ned Moore

3 Troop, 3 Commando, Worthing

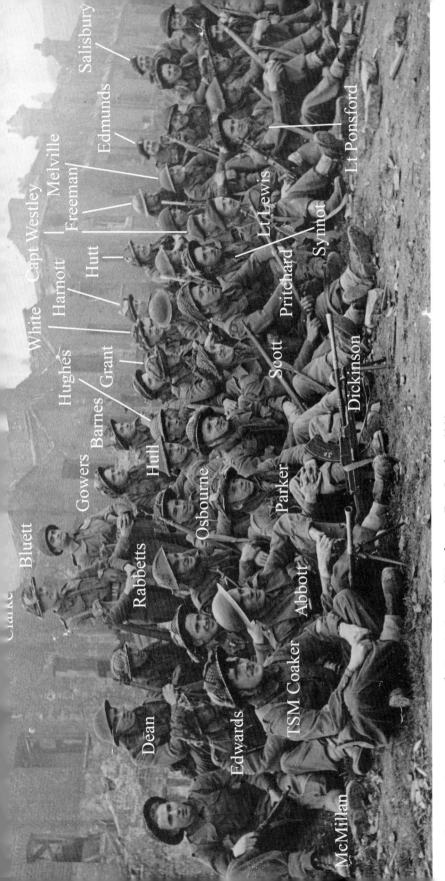

The Troop during training in the bombed area of Limehouse, East London, 1944

My sister Connie. This photo was
my lucky charm. The stains remain
from the water and marshland
encountered on D-Day

The Caen Canal (now Pegasus) Bridge
during the morning of D-Day

Howard's *Coup de Main* force of the 2nd Ox and Bucks that captured the Caen Canal Bridge. The three other graves are those of Fred Greenhalgh of the *Coup de Main* Party, killed during the landing of his assault glider; Peter Mercer-Wilson of No 4 Commando, shot by a sniper after crossing the bridge; and Arthur Charity of 6 Commando (*Imperial War Museum*)

AMFREVILLE — Bureau de Poste

Collection Bompain

Amfreville. The Post Office is just on the left. The hill up which 3 Troop advanced into enemy fire is beyond it to the right

The pond at Amfreville, which no longer exists, is now the site of the 3 Commando Memorial

pond in Amfreville

Chateau d'Amfreville

Fred Rabbetts and Tucker Jennings

The Saulnier Farm. It was just outside the entrance that Lord Lovat and Brigadier Hugh Kindersley, CO of the 6th Airlanding Brigade were badly wounded and Lieutenant Colonel Johnson, CO of the 12th Parachute Battalion was killed. The Saulnier family became great friends of the Commandos both during and after the war

Ellis Norris, Ted Pritchard and Dickinson

Outside the house where I spotted Selby. Johnny Johnson, Sgt Cassidy (?) Tucker Jennings, myself and Fennessey

n in 1945

Motorcycle Section, CMP

Jock Pearson and yours truly, CMP

gave him to me. Big Bill Garrett, the medic, had not arrived from the beach and somehow I had been given the first-aid kit. I couldn't do anything for Dixie. Within two minutes he was dead. He looked at me and ... gone. Then I bandaged Westley's wrist and put his elbow in a sling. A worried Paddy Harnett was saying to me, 'Have a look at me wedding tackle. Is me wedding tackle all right?' Much to his relief, it was.

The Lance-Sergeant, Les Hill, then said to Ossie, 'What about Johnny Abbott?' So the two of them went up the hill again. As they bent down to pick him up, the firing re-started and Hill was hit in the head. Abbott had to be left on the ground and Hill staggered back in a daze, dragging his weapon along the ground behind him. Blood was pouring down his face and someone said, 'He's a goner, there's nothing you can do for him.' He just carried straight on down to the bottom of the hill. A 9mm bullet had actually gone through the front of his helmet, parting his hair and leaving a furrow the size of an index finger across the top of his skull. He was one of the few men wearing a helmet and was only doing so because earlier it had been jangling against his bicycle. After the action, Ted Gowers helped him and Harnett to a First-Aid Post that had been set up at the bottom of the hill.[17]

Meanwhile, Ponsford, the surviving officer, had been on a recce and found a route around the back of the houses. He came back and explained what we were going to do. Synnott's Section was to cover the right hand side of the village, Salisbury the left. We had the job of going back up the bloody road again. On the signal we were just going to rush the village. The bloke who had first fired at us from the gable-end of the house must have thought that it was all over because it had gone quiet. He came out of a side door in the wall just as Tucker Jennings was approaching it. Jennings just blew him away. Then there was a big firefight. Everybody was letting go. 'Flash' Freeman did some good work with the 2-inch mortar. The village's post office, from which enemy fire was coming, was plastered with mortar bombs. Ponsford went to the right with his mob and the Troop swept through the village. The Germans made a very hasty

[17] I had Harnett's small pack afterwards because he had dumped it on the ground. There was not a stitch of Army kit in it. It was crammed tight with fags, and I didn't smoke!

exit to the east, towards Breville. Not a single man was lost in this second attack and about thirty prisoners were taken, a lot of these being Russians and Poles who fought until they saw it was all over and then stuck their hands up. Then it was, 'Polski, Polski,' but until a couple of ticks before, they were killing your mates. Hard luck, son.

We then discovered that some of the firing had not been from German weapons, but the 9 Para men who had come from Merville, and who had got into the grounds of a large building over on the left, the Chateau d'Amfreville. They had heard us and were doing their best to provide some covering fire.

Afterwards, we were standing on a T-Junction at the entrance to the chateau with the prisoners sitting along the wall. My old man had always said to me, 'Get away from Crossroads, T-Junctions, anything that can be put on a map, because it can be coordinated by artillery.' I was there with a couple of other lads looking at a Mannlicher semi-automatic rifle that Ted Pritchard had found when a German started running across the field. I said, 'Here, look!' and Ted took aim, BANG! Down went this bloke. Ted said, 'It works!' The next minute he reversed the weapon and smashed it over the wall because that was what we had been told to do. We had no idea if D-Day had been a success, so any captured German weapon was smashed up.

Just as we moved forward up a track on the other side of the road, Jerry started shelling the T-Junction. One of the first casualties was a horse standing there, which sank to its knees with a big gash in its side. A jeep came up from the mortar section and turned into the driveway to the Chateau. TSM Coker went over and began talking to the lads. Picking up a helmet from the jeep, he put it on his head and said, 'I'm all right now!', just as a shell landed and took half his head off. Billy Moore lost his arm and a couple of blokes in the jeep were injured, but the driver did the right thing and drove straight out of the area.

We took up position about fifty yards east of the town hall in a ditch that had a hedgerow on the bank and a large tree at the end. There was a good field of vision across a field full of cabbages for around a hundred yards, then a hedgerow and beyond that, an orchard.

*   *   *

Everybody had a brew up and something to eat. We each had two twenty-four hour ration packs which were rudimentary, but there were tins of Machonocie's M&V (meat and veg), and that was good stuff. The tin was pierced and put in hot water for ten minutes, although sometimes we had to eat it cold. There was also bacon wrapped in paper, that had to be pulled out of the tin. Some blokes would say, 'Eat the paper, throw away the bacon!' A lot of people scoffed at this compo, but if you were sensible and had the patience to prepare it correctly, using a mess tin, a decent meal could be had. Tea was made from a block that also contained milk and sugar. I gave that away to anybody who wanted it or swapped it for Oxo cubes as I preferred beef tea. Oxo mixed with broken biscuits was as good as soup.

I had dug down and forward into the bank of the ditch with Lance Corporal Jackie Barnes. The idea was that one person would keep watch on the edge while the other sat in the bank with a gas cape on him to get a bit of kip or have a brew up. If anything happened, all the bloke on watch had to do was kick the other on the head and he would come up straight away.

The end of the day arrived. D-Day had cost the Troop two out of the three officers, three of the four sergeants and the sergeant-major killed. Of the original seventy-five men, forty remained.

Chapter 8

Amfreville

First light arrived on D+1. It didn't need anyone to say 'Stand To', we were trained soldiers and knew what it meant. Everybody was watching out front but nothing happened, so some got their heads down, others had a brew and a bit of breakfast. As it became lighter so it started. With a terrific CRACK, a round went straight into a tree and another hit the bank. The Germans were firing rounds into the area in an attempt to find us, particularly the automatic weapon positions. Nobody returned fire. Commando soldiers are intelligent. When the firing abated Ponsford came up and said, 'Scott, get your Bren gun,' so I went and retrieved it from Parker, plus my .45 Colt automatic.

During the morning I also went back to the entrance of the Chateau d'Amfreville and picked up Coker's Thompson. His brains were all over it, so I went across the road to a pond by the post office and washed them away. The metalwork of the gun had been etched into, as if by acid.

Most casualties had been evacuated to the 6th Airborne ADS, but Dixie Dean was still lying there covered, and Abbot's booted and gaitered leg remained in the road. I went through the village collecting ammunition and anything that could be useful. We now knew that the Brigade was there to stay, whatever, so enemy weapons were also collected for use. I went back to our little corner. In the trench we had a Bren gun, a German Schmeisser, a rifle, Coker's Thompson and Jackie Barnes' personal weapon plus pistol and British and German grenades, so we were well stocked.

We decided to have a look around our immediate vicinity and found a dead Airborne Major in the hedgerow. The back of his leg

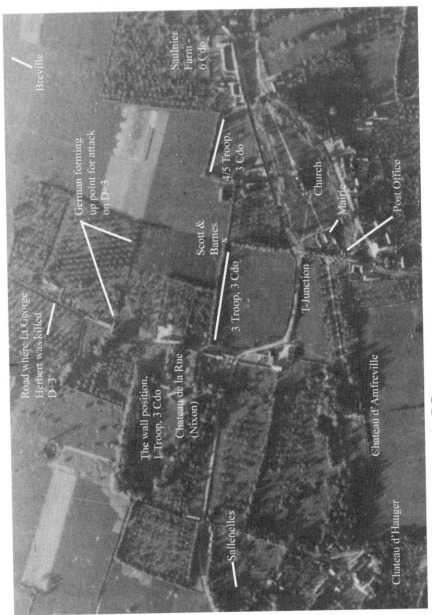

Commando positions immediately after D-Day.

had been blown away behind the knee. He had his large pack open and had tried to do something for himself by tying a towel around his leg. His wallet was out with a photo of his wife and two kids and he must have been looking at them when he died. Maybe if we had searched immediately on arrival he might still have been alive. It was just one of those things.

Patrolling began. One went out from our position and returned ten minutes later with a German prisoner. Two Commandos had him by the ankles and were dragging him along the floor!

In the early evening the remainder of 3 Commando arrived from Ranville and began to take up positions around us. 4 and 5 Troops had attacked the Merville Gun Battery during the afternoon and although they had entered the perimeter successfully, could not get past the locked doors of the casemates to deal with the guns. An artillery barrage had opened up on them, and enemy troops, supported by self-propelled guns, forced the Commandos to retire, suffering losses in the process.

*   *   *

The 6th Airborne Division had managed to form a defensive perimeter east of the River Orne and the 1st Special Service Brigade held part of the northern sector. To our immediate right was a mixture of 4 and 5 Troops of 3 Commando and to the far right at the end of Amfreville, 6 Commando was in the area around buildings of a farm owned by the Saulnier family. Forward and to the left was our 1 Troop, behind the high wall of another chateau, the Chateau de la Rue; 4 Commando was further north in Hauger and 45 Commando was three miles to the north in the Merville area. The Germans held Breville, causing a major problem for the Airborne perimeter, and ahead of us their front line stretched along the Gonneville Road then through Descanneville and the Merville Gun Battery to the coast. The distance between the different Commandos and the enemy varied, the closest being opposite Breville, around 700 yards away. Two farms were situated in No Man's Land, the Grande Ferme de Buisson to the north-east and Longuemare Farm, east of 1 Troop's wall position.

During the night of the 7th I was on watch and could hear constant rustling and movement to my left. I woke Jackie and we went to have a look. Moving a short distance, I pushed myself through the hedge and could see a body lying there. We thought, 'Is that someone crawling?' Jackie went and found Sergeant Synnott. He was a good lad and said, 'One of you cover me.' He found it to be the Airborne Major. Without telling us, someone on the left had decided to get rid of his body and pushed him out in front of the position, which was wrong. He was taken away. So that alarm was over.

The morning of 8 June duly arrived. This was the day we began to feel the strain, having been up all day on the 5th, all day on the 6th and without much rest on the 7th. Three days without proper food or sleep. However, up until now nothing had happened. The enemy had continued to try and find us, shelling and mortaring the area but still didn't know exactly where we were. And then it really started, heavy shelling. Everybody got their heads down. They seemed to be targeting the hedgerow in front and after a while Jackie Barnes said, 'Have a look.' I said, 'No, you have a look.' 'They might be coming.' 'Not while they're shelling.' So he said, 'I'll tell you what, we'll both have a look!' Nothing was happening, so we got down again. The fire then lengthened and moved away from the hedgerow, over our heads onto the road behind and the wall of the Chateau d'Amfreville. We looked again. Germans were now coming through the orchard and we could see these silly sods trying to line up behind the hedgerow. Where had I seen such stupidity before? The Black Watch assault on the 70th Suffolks. So now we had about a hundred yards between us and them. Word came down the line, 'No firing until the blast of the whistle.' There was none of this 'No. 1 group, 500' fire orders or anything like that, the stuff taught at Infantry Training School, you could see your targets in front of you! All the weapons were ready. The Germans then began to push their way through the hedgerow and form a ragged skirmish line. I suppose they were doing as ordered. They started to come through the cabbages and I began to wonder, 'Are you going to blow that bloody whistle or not?!' Ponsford let them get about halfway across the field, blew his whistle and everyone opened up. There was no question of reloading, we just threw one weapon down and picked up another, it didn't matter whether it was German or British. It felt like a lifetime, but after a couple of minutes they were all gone. Some

78

tried to run back. Too bad. We were looking at a field of busted cabbages and bodies.

That night, we went out front and knocked all the cabbages down to deny the enemy any cover whatsoever.

On the 9 June Jackie was having a doze and I was sitting in the hedge, keeping watch, well covered and out of sight. Suddenly, someone took a pot shot at our position and hit a stone or something hard in the bank. I felt a pain in the middle of my breastbone. Christ did it sting! I ripped open my blouse to reveal a shining sliver of metal sticking out of my chest. It looked like a bullet had shattered. I pulled it out, which didn't hurt too much, but it bled a little and I washed the cut. Better out than in. Jackie Barnes said, 'It's nothing to worry about,' so I just carried on. Had a sniper spotted us? After that I kept my head down.

The following morning, two Lloyd carriers came up and stopped behind us on the bend in the road. They belonged to the 51st Highland Division or 'Highway Decorators' as we called them, because they put their HD sign up all over the place. They began to off-load a couple of mortars and we sat there watching them set up, thinking, 'No. Surely you're not going to do that!' Out came the ammunition and they started firing, outgoing mail, straight to Jerry. Next thing, they had dismantled the mortars, got back in the carriers and sped away. What did we say? 'Get your heads down!' Jerry smashed the place. One of our men, Hodges, had dug his slit trench alongside a wall. A shell hit the wall and he got a lot of splinters down his back. Someone yelled out, 'Stretcher-bearers!' He was a pal of the medic, Bill Garrett, who was a big sod of about six foot three and built like two brick outhouses. Big Bill got there with a stretcher and he and another bloke pulled Hodges out of the hole and onto it. It was pandemonium with all the explosions around us, so the only way of getting to the First Aid station was to follow the hedgerows to the T-Junction. Such explosions are not like those shown in films when you hear a shell coming, because if it's near you, you don't hear it. That's what happened. Just as he got to the corner behind us, a shell hit our tree and they had to go to ground. Hodges fell off the stretcher. They got up, dumped him back on the stretcher and by this time Bill was screaming, 'Run, run, run. Get him down to the First Aid station,' but we knew Hodges was condemned because some of his organs were still lying on the ground.

3 Troop held that hedge for five days before being relieved by 5 Troop. It seemed longer. The hedgerow was a complete shambles, like something out of the '14–'18 War. Food was scarce and we had survived the week on our two ration packs and whatever could be scrounged. There were thirty of us left, all ranks.

We were moved to an orchard in the grounds at the rear of the Chateau d'Amfreville, about 500 yards behind the front line. There was a big German trench there and our instructions were to improve it, build some head cover and get a good night's sleep, so we tried to make the trench as comfortable as possible. We thought that the Chateau must have a wine cellar, but as hard as we searched, could find nothing. However, someone did 'find' a calf and as Jackie Barnes and Spencer were butchers, between them they strung it up, killed it, gutted it and we had fresh meat that night.

In the morning, everybody went over to the pond, had a wash, shave and then a good breakfast, 'interior economy' as the Army called it. In the afternoon came the crunch. We found that the Troop, from that point on, was to be sent out on patrols each night.

It was necessary to patrol to dominate the ground and maintain the initiative. To achieve this there were several types of patrol, beginning with a Reconnaissance Patrol. If something worthwhile was discovered, a Standing Patrol would then be sent out to confirm it, followed by a Fighting Patrol to carry out a raid. There were also Liaison Patrols where a certain distance existed between units, as contact had to be maintained.

The favourite number of men for a Recce patrol was five, all lightly armed and clad. The patrol leader's four men each had a job to do, such as navigator, and a pacer who judged distance by counting the number of his own paces, knowing how many represented a certain distance. If in some instances it was necessary to take a prisoner, two of the men could be detailed as a 'snatch party'. They all watched the patrol leader, he did not watch them. He was the one who gave the signals using four fingers of one hand. No noise was made, you went out and came back without the enemy knowing you had paid them a visit.

Standing Patrols moved out at first darkness, took up position as near to the enemy as possible and lay there all night to look and listen. If there were fifteen men, they would spread out around three feet apart and so cover a front of about forty-five yards. You had to recognize sounds like digging, lighting up fags, anything that gave away the enemy positions, even people farting! Again, get in and out without being known.

The Fighting or Raiding Patrol was exactly that. You had gained information, so now act on it, create the maximum amount of damage and disruption. It could be a Troop, half a Troop, heavily armed, all short-range offensive weapons like Thompson sub-machine guns. The planners told you what time to start out and where they wanted you to go, but did not stipulate what time to come back because you never knew what was going to happen. If possible, the patrol would infiltrate between the enemy's advanced posts, pass through the Jerry lines and do the job coming back out. Behind the German lines you had a certain freedom of movement because they would be looking towards our lines. You were then hitting Jerry from behind and also while on your way back. For obvious reasons a patrol's path out was never the route by which it returned.

No. 10 Commando consisted entirely of men who came from Nazi-occupied countries. These were organized into Troops comprising specific nationalities. For example, 'X' Troop was for Germans. We had a couple of German Jews from the Troop, called Lawrence and Spencer (their adopted English names). I did a couple of jobs with both of them. Spencer impressed me most because if there was a cold-blooded soldier, he had to be it. On the night of 12/13 June, volunteers from the Troop formed part of a large 3 Commando fighting patrol. Starting out at 2145 hours, it went straight to the Grande Ferme de Buisson, which had been taken during the afternoon. This was our raiding base. Over to the right, men of the 6th Airborne Division had begun an assault on the village of Breville, and a considerable quantity of enemy guns firing tracer could be seen on that flank. Under cover of darkness we moved forward until halting about a hundred yards short of the main Gonneville – Breville road and 400 yards outside Gonneville itself. The patrol split here and Lieutenant Ponsford took four of us including Spencer as interpreter, to the right. Under covering fire, if required, we were to push on to the road, ambush some Germans and bring back a couple of prisoners. We went down the road and Spencer signalled with his hand 'One, two and three, get down.' No talking, down, watch. He took Ted Pritchard and myself and we just walked normally along the side of the road. If you started to creep

81

or crouch and the enemy saw you, they would know something was up, whereas they would not think anything of someone walking about as if in their own area. All of a sudden we could hear the faint sound of snoring, and approached it. I got on one side and Pritchard the other. We bent down, got hold of this bloke and pulled him bodily out of a hole. He stood there and Spencer pushed the barrel of his Thompson into the German's guts. He said, 'Du bist gefangener.' The bloke must have thought that his mates were playing a joke! I guess he said something like, 'Don't play about!' and pushed the Thompson away. Most of us carried a knife on our thigh, in a special attachment on our trousers (some had a pocket inside as well). Spencer said, 'I'm not playing about,' and went straight in with his knife. The bloke just collapsed back into the hole.

We carried on along the road and found another Jerry, but this one was sensible. He was grabbed, pulled out and didn't need any telling. He took one look and knew who had got hold of him. Spencer made him pick up all his gear and we went back down the road, where he picked up all the dead German's equipment. Then he got the body out of the hole and Spencer said, 'Put him across the back of your shoulders,' so he had two lots of gear and the body to carry. We got back to the other two and then returned to the Grande Ferme de Buisson, dumped the body and made our way to Amfreville along a back lane. Afterwards, I asked Spencer about the first German. 'Christ, was that necessary?' He said, 'The next thing that bloke would have done was start shouting. We'd have all been up the creek. And you can't leave them behind because they'll know we've been.' 'But they'll know anyway.' 'No. All they're going to find is two empty holes. They won't be sure, 'cos if we'd have left all their rifles and kit behind, they'd know that we had got them.' That was Spencer.

The other one, Lawrence, would for example, walk across the cornfield to the Grande Ferme de Buisson with a bloke as a sort of minder. He would drop the minder off saying, 'Wait for me here,' continue toward the German positions and talk to them, saying things like, 'The war's finished, you might as well give in now. Come over and get some decent food!' He would bring prisoners back like that.

* * *

The 6th Airborne's assault on Breville proved costly, but the village was taken and the gap in the northern part of the defensive perimeter closed. Unfortunately, during the pre-assault barrage on the village, some of it had fallen short, severely wounding Lord Lovat and a number of other high-ranking officers. The CO of 6 Commando, Derek Mills-Roberts, assumed command of the Brigade.

On 13 June at 1630 hours Jimmy Synnott led twelve of us on a reinforced recce patrol to hold the Grande Ferme de Buisson. There was no trouble on the way out and Jimmy positioned us around the farm. All we had to do was lie low, watch, listen and take note. Sure enough, later, a party of approximately forty Germans could be seen approaching. They began to circle the farm and we kept quiet in the farmhouse. I was kneeling below a window and Synnott looked over to see a German standing immediately outside. Jimmy didn't know whether to warn me or not, but my head was well down below the window so he said nothing. Luckily for us the Germans had only moved in on three sides, so it was decided to quietly move up the track using cover and get out via the front gate. We had just started on our way when there was the sound of aircraft. Bombs began to land all around, luckily only light ones, maybe 250 lb types, but the noise, dust and debris flying about was terrific. A watchman's hut made of railway sleepers at the track T-Junction was reduced to matchwood, but again our luck held as there were no casualties and we all returned safely. It was the USAAF, friendly fire indeed!

Two days later, we carried out a patrol to find lines of approach to the village of Sallenelles. Leaving the orchard behind the Chateau d'Amfreville, we proceeded along a covered track to Hauger. The track ended at the Chateau in Hauger, so we turned right towards the Sallenelles Road, passing through the defensive positions of 4 Commando at the T-Junction, a leading edge of woodland, then an open field on our left. We came under indirect machine gun fire and so started to take cover in the edge of the wood, when there was a solitary BANG! At first I thought, 'Mortar bomb', but then, 'One bomb?' A face appeared through the bushes and said, 'Oi! You're in our minefield.' Lieutenant Ponsford ordered everyone to stand still. Fred Rabbetts had trodden on a 75 Hawkins grenade. After checking that Fred was dead – a right bloody mess too – we extricated ourselves by treading in the footprints that led in. Needless to say, the patrol was over. The next job was to get Fred out of there. Luckily someone else got that task.

* * *

On D-Day a kid called 'Whitey' had been moving along beside the wall of the Chateau d'Amfreville just as an 88 mm round hit the top of it. The concussion sent him bomb-happy. Any bang and it was terrible to see a bloke like that. He was still with us, but had been put in what we called the 'Todt Organisation', burying the dead. Every night when the Troop went out on a job, someone had to stay with him and on one particular night it was me. I was with Whitey in the big trench that ran along the wall of the Chateau. We had collapsed part of it over the trench to make a roof, so there was only a small space to get in. Inside we had a German MG42 facing straight down the track leading to Hauger. That was the only way into the position. Somebody else guarded the other direction. After a while I said to him, 'I'm not half thirsty. Go and find something to drink.' He came back, got in the hole and gave me a bottle. Thanking him, I pulled the cork out and took a large swig. 'Jesus!' He had come back with a bottle of Calvados! That was only the start of the evening.

Later on, the inevitable happened. The Germans started their nightly hate, a regular artillery barrage, all around the position. Whitey went absolutely berserk and I couldn't hold him. He pushed the gun out of the way and ran straight down the track into a small wood, just as a salvo exploded in the trees. I thought that he must surely have been killed. In the morning the patrol came back and I explained to Ponsford that I just couldn't hold him. He said, 'Well, we did what we could.'

Three days later, Ponsford decided to have a look in the part of the trench that went through the small wood. By then the wood consisted largely of fallen branches and cut-up trees. He went right to the end of the trench and found a body. It was Whitey, bunched up like a dead rabbit, still alive but he just wouldn't come out. He had had nothing to eat or drink since the night I lost him. The kid was shattered. Ponsford came back, got hold of a couple of the Guardsmen, big boys and they went in and literally dragged him out. He was taken into Commando Headquarters but Ned Moore couldn't do a thing for him. He just had to be sedated and evacuated. It was the worse case of shell shock I ever saw.

* * *

One day I found an outhouse in the woods to the east of the main chateau building. In it was a massive cider press that had a big screw. Then I noticed a little door in a corner and so smashed the padlock off and went in. It was the wine cellar! The pigeon-holes were full of wine. When I told the lads, they were taking bottles, tasting them, 'Don't like that one,' and smashing them. It didn't last long. A complete waste. God knows how much it was worth.

There was also a big vat of cider. We left a round, fifty-cigarette tin beside it as a drinking vessel for whenever anyone fancied a bevvy. It was good cider.

* * *

On the night of 22/23 June a couple of small patrols went out. One of them, comprising three men, was led by Corporal Lawrence, the German Jew, with Lance-Corporal Littler and Trooper Young. They were detailed to get a prisoner. Lawrence gave instructions that he would creep forward and as usual try to get one by persuading him to come quietly. If he was detected and fired upon, everyone was to make their own getaway. After moving forward, Littler saw Lawrence kneel beside a trench and start speaking to a German. Lawrence then shot him with one bullet from his Tommy gun. The German screamed and a machine gun opened fire as a party of the enemy ran to the scene. Lawrence appeared to be trying to get the German's paybook from his pocket. A further machine gun opened fire, so Littler and Young split up and headed back to a hedgerow. They waited for Lawrence but he didn't return. We never saw him again.

That same night, we attempted an ambush on Jerry by trying to deceive him into coming out to help supposed comrades. A firefight was to be staged between two Commando patrols, one using enemy weapons, the other British. It had been carefully planned where the patrols were to be positioned, where to fire and for how long. We were the British patrol and had three Bren guns in a ditch in front of the Grande Ferme de Buisson, while the 'German' patrol took up position on the other side of the Gonneville Road, leaving us at right angles to each other. At 2355 hours we opened up and the other patrol returned fire. This went on for about ten minutes. However, Jerry guessed what was going on and we received some 'golden rain', tracers going over the top, peppering the farm. For the next hour, flares went up and both patrols were fired on but returned without incident. For some reason, of the three Bren guns, the only one to fire had been mine. Ellis Norris had had a problem with his. When we got back Ponsford asked him why the Bren had not fired. Ellis said, 'I carried out all the IAs [Instant actions, i.e. checks for basic stoppages], everything, but it just wouldn't fire.' 'Get that bloody gun stripped down, I want to have a look at it.' They found that he had forgotten to put the firing pin back in. That should have been instant dismissal back to the Guards, but Ponsford said, 'No harm came of it, don't do that again.' Ellis must have been tired and it was just one of those things.[18] If Ponsford had RTU'd him, he would have been getting rid of a good soldier. He was not going to get a replacement anyway and at that time we must have been down to about twenty-eight men, all ranks.

Such tiredness was a big problem as we were still not getting much sleep. There were normal duties during the day, Standing To at first light, Standing To at night. If you did not go out on patrol you did STAG back at the base. I went on a patrol with Lieutenant Neil Thompson, along the hedgerow to the left of the Grande Ferme de Buisson and was dropped off with Ronnie Bridges, my No. 2 for it, while the others went on. I had got down behind the gun and the next thing I knew someone was kicking my feet. 'Come on Scotty, we're out.' I had fallen asleep. They had shot two Germans on that patrol and I knew nothing about it. Ronnie Bridges must have fallen asleep as well. A complete gun crew out of it, no good to anyone.

Besides the patrolling there were also night OP duties to carry out. Everyone did it in rotation. To help keep you awake the hole dug for the OP was deep, round and the diameter was such that you had to stand up. During enemy bombing raids the flak from the beachhead could be seen wriggling about like waves, I suppose when they tipped the barrels up and down. However, the Germans dropped

---

[18] We never found out why the other one didn't fire.

their bombs anywhere because once past the canal bridge, with the amount of men and materiel about, they had to hit something.

In the region of Honfleur a big railway gun would fire day and night. During darkness, from the OP you could see a flash and a whistle, and then an explosion somewhere on the beaches. A compass was provided with which to take a bearing on the flash as quickly as possible. If it fired again, another bearing was taken and marked down. In the morning these would be coordinated with those of previous nights. In the end its position was worked out, Typhoons were sent in and they successfully 'pranged' it.

* * *

The patrolling continued. Jimmy Synnott took us on another night-time job towards the Longuemare Farm to obtain a couple of prisoners. Whether it was just bad luck I don't know, but halfway up the road we were caught in the open by a mortar stonk. In such a situation you don't stay there and take cover, you get out of it. I ran back down the road, reached a house and saw that the front door was open. I jumped in, went down about three small steps and came face to face with two Germans. One was standing there with a rifle, the other with a Schmeisser MP40 sub-machine gun. I don't know who was the more surprised, but before I knew what had happened they had thrown their weapons away and put their hands up! So I walked out of the house with two prisoners. Their paybooks identified them as Obergefreiter Julius Haag and Gefreiter Hermann Lehmann.

A 20 mm multi-barrelled anti-aircraft gun began to annoy us at night. It would come up to the road and track junction of the Longuemare Farm and begin to blatter off along the line held by 3 and 6 Commandos. Starting with the wall position, it would work its way round to the Saulnier Farm and back again, then pack it in and go somewhere else. This went on until one night Bungy Young decided he had had enough. The next night a patrol was sent out to await its arrival and then proceeded to wipe out the whole crew and the accompanying defence section as well.

During the night of 26/27 June two Assault Sections went out to raid a German position on the Gonneville road. I was in the Support Section in a bomb crater just off the road. Our job was counter-fire.

When any German MGs opened up the flashes could be seen, so we would fire at that locality to keep their heads down. Keith Ponsford went in with a Section, left, onto the road, Eddie Edwards took a Section to the right. The first sounds we heard involved Eddie's Section. There was a hell of a shindig for a minute or two, then it was quiet. Then it started on the left. An MG opened up and being on the left-hand side of the Support Section, I gave it a burst. As mentioned before, I did not play around firing five round bursts. I wanted to get Jerry down, so I gave him the magazine. It didn't take long to fire a magazine and I had hardly finished when the mud in front of me erupted. It was either a grenade or a mortar bomb but it was right on target. Thinking, 'Sod this,' I moved to the other side of the crater with Ronnie Bridges. Next thing, Ponsford was pounding back across the field and jumped into the crater. Then more bodies were coming back, again, straight into the crater. By this time, the German defensive fire was coming down and when Jerry let go, he let go! The whole bloody Gonneville Road was coming alive. It had gone pear-shaped and there was only one thing to do. Get out. Ponsford said, 'Right. All up. Get out.' I asked Bridges for the spare magazines and he put them down. I said, 'Get out of it,' and started firing from one side to the other, letting off anywhere. I think I had gone, lost 'my north' a little bit! I kept going until they were all clear and the ammunition expended. So there I was with the Bren and a pile of empty magazines. All I had left was a Colt and my knife. I suddenly thought, 'Oh blimey, come back dear earth! What do I do now?' I knew the general direction to go, into the big cornfield behind. I didn't like Army overcoats but that night it was raining and I had gone out wearing one. It was the first thing ditched. I also had to leave some of the empty mags behind because I couldn't put them anywhere. I got out of the hole and began crawling with the Bren through the standing corn, which was pretty high. Eventually I realized that I didn't know which way I was going. I had no sense of direction and so for the rest of the night just lay there getting soaked.

I calculated that as soon as daylight arrived, barrage balloons would be raised on the beachhead to help protect the ships and that would give me an indication of direction. Eventually first light arrived and up they came. I started crawling through the corn and came out of the field. There was a crack over my head. I had moved to the wrong side of the field. Someone must have been alert and let go. I got back into the corn and thought, 'Well that was silly. Now Jerry knows there is still someone in here.' I crawled off again in what I now thought was the right direction. I came out the other side and got a burst of MG fire! I lay there for a bit and thought again. 'This is ridiculous. Let's get my position for God's sake.' Having done this, I came out into a sweet-pea field that was familiar, and moving through this I eventually saw the buildings of the Grande Ferme de Buisson. There was a hedge and beyond it an orchard that ran into the side of the farm at the end of what was known as Dead Man's Wood. Unfortunately, from the edge of the sweet-peas it was just flat plain grass, no cover, nothing for seventy-five yards. 'What am I going to do? If I crawl across this slowly, Jerry will see me and what sort of a target am I going to make? Or shall I up, run and dive over the hedge?' Being impulsive, I decided to run. However, I realized the Bren was 23 lb of useless weight, so I stripped it down and put the gas regulator, firing pin and spring, extractor, stay and spring and trigger group in my pocket. I then distributed the barrel, the body group and bipod to the winds so that there was no way the Germans could use the weapon. I ran and dived over the hedge into the orchard and then from one tree to the other, into the back of the farm. Nothing happened. A Royal Marine came out of the farm and as I got nearer, just put my hands up. He gave me the signal 'Come in' and approaching him I started talking, '3 Troop, 3 Commando. We got stuck on a bleedin' job last night.' He said, 'We've heard about you. Anybody else out there?' I said, 'How do I know? As far as I know, I'm the last one in.' He took me into the farmhouse and I found that they were a Standing Patrol. An officer asked me if I was all right, gave me a fag (the one time I did have a smoke), half a cup of tea, a lump of chocolate and we sat there having a natter. Then I walked back to the Commando lines which was nearly another mile and went into 3 Troop's HQ behind the Chateau d'Amfreville. The reaction was, 'Good Lord, look who's turned up!' All of my kit had been distributed amongst the others. It was normal procedure. If you were gone, you didn't need it anymore. I did get it all back though. Lieutenant Ponsford said, 'A telegram has already been sent to say you're missing. You'd better go and see Bungy. He will want to know all about last night.' So I gave Peter Young a complete report of what had happened and he said, 'Right. And the gun?' 'Well, I stripped it down and threw it away.' He said, 'A very careless soldier. Go back out there and find that gun. Take Corporal Grant with you.' The telegram had already gone, so that night I wrote a hurried letter to my mother. The next day I found Grant, one of our sniping corporals, and told him what Bungy had said. Granty asked if I had any idea where it could be, and I told him that I could get back to where I threw the bits and pieces. The route we took was not the same way that I had returned, but to the left of the farm and then into the cornfield. Even so, we must have been spotted because Jerry started amusing himself by lobbing 81 mm mortar bombs at us. We moved individually, covering each other, but after any movement, a couple of bombs would arrive. Jerry only had to get one on target. In the end Granty said, 'Sod this, Scotty, let's get out of here.'[19]

*   *   *

A Reconnaissance Patrol was formed comprising Jimmy Synnott, Jackie Barnes, Ellis Norris, Ted Pritchard and myself. Our orders were to search the area between Sallenelles, the Merville Battery and the Grande Ferme de Buisson. Also, previous patrols had noticed that a 'Goulash Kannon', a German Field Kitchen, seemed to make regular appearances on the road between Franceville Plage and Merville. This was to be confirmed. If required, the patrol was to stay out all night.

The ETD, ETA and password were provided and everyone was made aware of their individual duties. Our attire was cap comforter, Para smock, denim trousers and SV (Sole Vibram) rubber-soled Commando boots or gym shoes. We were only lightly armed with either Thompsons or rifles, fifty rounds per man, plus smoke and HE grenades. Personal camouflage was completed, weapons and ammunition cleaned and checked, and all traces of identity, both personal and unit, removed. We then had a rest before setting off in the early afternoon.

From the orchard at the rear of the Chateau d'Amfreville we passed along the wooded track to the Chateau at Hauger, then turned right to the T-Junction with the road to Sallenelles. Having

[19] After the War I mentioned this incident to Peter Young saying, 'You made me go out and get that bloody gun.' He said, 'What! I was only joking you bloody fool!'

90

very carefully crossed the road we proceeded downhill, following a small track, but not actually on the path. After descending for about 350 yards the patrol turned right and passed between two bungalows, both camouflaged enemy blockhouses, but empty. We were now heading towards the Merville Battery. All was quiet. Eventually, we came across a lane from the Grande Ferme de Buisson. An orchard there had been bombarded by our Air Force with baskets full of shells for the 75 mm guns of the Airborne artillery. There were parachutes all over the place, some on, some off the baskets.

Here the patrol turned left in the direction of Franceville Plage. Another 500 yards and we were in position on the main Sallenelles–Merville road, just opposite a small copse. All this had taken time due to careful fieldcraft and with hardly a word spoken. We knew that enemy artillery and infantry were around there. Across the road was the reported site for feeding time. It was a good, covered position.

Two well-concealed men were assigned to observe while the rest of us took up all-round defence. At around 2100 hours, iron-shod wheels and horses' hooves could be heard approaching from the direction of Merville. Shortly after, a 'Goulash Kannon' arrived and turned down the track into the copse, where we presumed the cooks would prepare and serve the evening meal.

About half an hour later the troops began to arrive. Mess tins were clanging, conversations and laughter were going on and the lighting of cigarettes could be seen. Strange for Jerry, but he must have felt safe.

The information had been confirmed, so very carefully we retired. Jimmy Synnott chose the route, straight along the Sallenelles road! Crazy? Not really. When troops of any nation have food, no one seems to take heed, so we left Jerry to his feeding, blissfully unaware that ten eyes and ears had been logging their movements. Back in Amfreville we were debriefed and the information supplied to the Intelligence Officer. The result was a fighting patrol two nights later led by Lieutenant Colonel Peter Young himself.

3 Troop supplied the men, and we all made our separate ways to the location. 'A' Section, about ten men, took up position in extended order to the left and at right angles to the Merville road. Jackie Barnes and myself were forward in the ditch on the right-hand side of the road, armed with Thompsons on which we had

taped two mags together, but in opposite directions. Up on the right was a Bren Section to provide covering fire for the withdrawal. We waited. Sure enough along came the Goulash Kannon and out came the men to eat. The jeep, with Christopher driving and Peter Young himself on the .50 Browning, went straight up the road, entered the copse and Bungy let rip into the crowd. When the belt was finished they reversed out and to cover them, Jackie Barnes and myself stood up and began firing into the mêlée. When the first mag was empty we turned the taped magazines up the other way, continued firing and then moved back. 'A' Section took over, continuing to fire into the panic and covering us out. Then the Bren Section covered 'A' Section out. Bungy gave Jackie and myself a ride back as escorts and we all moved straight back up the hill to Amfreville.

3 Troop did another such raid on a house at the Merville Battery. It was a night-time job, again acting on information. It had been found that the Germans were using one of the houses next to the Battery as a 'Doss House', I suppose to get out for a bit of grub and a kip. We went out to the Grande Ferme de Buisson and 'snurgled' or crawled through the enemy front lines over the Gonneville road. Then moved north, around the back of the site, and up the entrance road to the Battery. On reaching the house some blokes were sent forward to prepare to open the shutters, others were ready with hand grenades and I was put in position opposite the front door. On the given signal the shutters were opened, grenades thrown through the windows, the front door kicked open and I just emptied a full magazine into the house. Then we were out, moving to the west, the opposite direction to which we had come. We did not know who or how many were in there, or what damage had been done, but would wait for reports coming through and might hear a couple of days later.

* * *

3 Troop was sitting around in our orchard behind Commando HQ. Mortars and artillery were going off in the vicinity, but we were quite bored. Some people were cleaning weapons, others cooking (we were always hungry), some listening to a made-up radio. We all knew that come nightfall we would be on another patrol, and so took the opportunity to chat, smoke, clean up and relax.

Suddenly a van came around the corner by our pond. A man got out and pushed up a side shutter. It was a Salvation Army mobile canteen! 'Christ, what are they doing here?' They commenced to dole out tea, buns and fags, and the lads were of course delighted. I went over to speak to the man who appeared to be in charge. 'Do you know where you are?' 'Somewhere in Normandy called Amfreville.' 'OK,' I said, 'Behind you, that Chateau is 3 Commando HQ. This orchard is 3 Troop's position and the house that you can see through those bushes, 300 yards away, is occupied by the Germans.' 'Oh is it?' said the Sally Army man. 'You had better go and get them. Maybe they would like a cup of tea as well!' The men choked on their buns with laughter. Afterwards, the mobile canteen reversed around the corner and disappeared down the drive towards Ranville perhaps, but wherever, to brighten the lives of other squaddies.

* * *

By July, only a month after our arrival, all of us were now so-called veterans. If that meant being reasonably dirty, tired, hungry and slightly bomb-happy, we qualified. I had found that the whole experience of being in action began after the briefing for a patrol. While you prepared and had a bite to eat, there was a sense of apprehension without actually being scared; just a feeling, a form of tension. You relied on your mates, and as they would be talking or joking, you would try and do the same.

Once in action, you were tired but switched on, alert. If it was an advance to contact situation, initially there would not be too much imagination, but as you advanced the expectancy got worse. If shells or mortar bombs started to arrive it was impersonal; however, when machine guns opened up, it became personal. There was an immediate feeling of shock, 'Where is it coming from? Casualties?', but if you were OK, keep going forward, remaining wary. Then someone zoomed in on the enemy positions, you started to fire back and the action had begun for real. Orders would follow and once set and ready, the apprehension seemed to evaporate, but even then you were thinking, 'I'm blapping off, but it's going to come back.' You were not going to fire at the enemy without him answering!

If in the open and quite a distance from the objective, it was get down and firefight. If we were too near, that is if the enemy opened

93

fire late, it was rush in and open fire to keep their heads down, spoil their aim.

From the defensive aspect if you were in a position or slit trench, the attackers had the problem. They were out in the open, but we had to keep cool, wait until they got to the point of no return and then open fire. It could be said that action is fifty percent oblivion, you just react by instinct.

The most dangerous period was afterwards. A weariness tended to creep in, but you had to keep alert, because that was the time when the Germans loved to counter-attack.

Some people were found to be gun-shy because pointing a gun at a target is totally different to actually aiming at a person. That is the difference between troops. Some might be good during training, but when you came under fire, that was when it mattered.

In action you were either giving it or taking it. One you endure, but the other, have no conscience. If you fired a bullet, bomb or mortar, it was to kill someone. For them, tough.

* * *

Our casualties had been high and we had had two or three lots of replacements, although one group came from the disbanded Beach Groups. The poor sods never knew what hit them.

The routine of patrolling and dominating the ground continued well into August but on the 18th we finally moved off, to the Bois de Bavent.

Chapter 9

The Bois de Bavent and the Breakout

3 Commando was to relieve a Parachute Battalion in the Bavent Wood, a few hundred yards north-east of the Le Mesnil brickworks. When we arrived the only way into the position was through a narrow gap in a hedgerow, and only two men could move in as two moved out, so 3 Troop had to line the hedges while the changeover took place. It was situated near an infamous T-Junction, where the main road to Varaville met the turn-off for the village of Bavent. Ted Pritchard, Ellis Norris and myself realized that our Section was going to be one of the last to get through, so we moved into a small wood, got a fire going and made a cup of tea. With all the movement the Germans must have realized something was going on because a sudden mortar stonk landed on the junction. One of the first casualties was Jackie Barnes. An 81 mm mortar bomb landed just in front of him and he was peppered with shrapnel from head to toe. He looked like a pound of mincemeat. Everybody helped to get rid of the casualties and eventually he was put onto a stretcher and taken away.[20]

Finally, we moved into our position. The first men along the hedge that led to the wood were the Vickers Medium Machine Gun Section, and we were between them and the next hedgerow. The enemy had mined the field behind us, and in a corner Marine Commando engineers were digging out an unexploded German bomb.

[20] He survived, but every year he was back in hospital having lumps of iron taken out of him.

95

A parachutist had built the dugout that I inherited. The roof was made of empty equipment containers filled with earth and covered with more earth on top. Jerry mortared us at any time, day or night. All you could do was get to the bottom of the slit trench, make yourself small and just hope that one didn't drop straight in, although we always made some head cover because you had a better chance of avoiding injury, or worse. During a stonk, three 81 mm bombs landed on or very near my dugout. I was shook up, dazed and deafened but OK, thanks to one unknown Para.

My dugout was the nearest the cookhouse. I say cookhouse, but it was just a ditch where they cooked the grub! This had an obvious advantage but also a big disadvantage. At most times someone would be there getting a bit of food, and when the mortaring started, where was the first place they jumped? Into my bloody hole! I was forever shovelling out spilt dinners.

We found the Bois de Bavent to be an eerie place because you could walk down the rides all morning and not see a soul, then in the afternoon, step two yards inside the wood and bump straight into a German patrol.

In the no man's land in front of our position was a place called Hinds Farm and about forty yards from it a couple of our listening posts had been established. When on duty there, if any noise was heard you looked through a little handheld periscope to check the buildings. If someone was moving about you got beneath a blanket and gave three turns on the handle of a radio set. You didn't actually speak, but just caused three rings. This signal called in a mortar or artillery barrage on the farm. Sometimes people could be heard screaming, but fifteen minutes later, the Germans would be back in there. They never gave up.

All kinds of little irritations were devised just to make life a little bit more uncomfortable. Jerry did the same. One of ours was an electrically fired .50 Browning and a loud speaker set up in the hedgerow. Sometimes a German-speaking Commando would come up, get in the dugout, pick up the microphone and tell them the usual stuff, 'Give up, you will be well fed.' If there was no answer, he would give them a couple of bursts on the Browning. In the trees further down the hedgerow was a gauze mask, like a pumpkin for Halloween night and a Mk V Airborne Sten with a cocked magazine positioned beside it. At night the pumpkin would be lit up, the

Germans given enough time to notice it and then a string pulled to fire a couple of bursts! The only problem was that every so often someone had to get up there and change the magazine! This all became routine until one day we were told to get ready to move forward. Finally, it was the breakout from the beachhead. In front of us was a supposed German minefield. However, we had our doubts because everyone, with morbid curiosity and amusement, had watched when a donkey had strayed into the field, waiting for it to be blown up! Nothing happened. When we came to clear a path through the minefield, it was found that the Germans had buried pots and pans!

Passing through the village of Bavent a German was found half-submerged in the roadside ditch. We got him out and kicked his arse down the road. The Commando moved on to Petiville, then Varaville, where a Para was still hanging in a tree, directly opposite a German ack-ack position. He had been there since D-Day. Some of the Airborne lads who came up after us cut him down. We decided to take up residence in the ack-ack position, but then Ted Pritchard said, 'Scotty, there's something funny in here. I don't like it.' As booby-traps were part of my job, I went and looked around. The dugouts were very well made. The Germans had lined the walls and floor with doors from the surrounding houses. Mattresses, sheets and blankets lay on the floor. The bed was neatly made and turned back. Very inviting. A little gap in the doors in the back wall was apparent and I could see cotton going between them. One of the floorboard doors was resting slightly up on another and I thought, 'It's for someone to step on, that's going to be a pressure switch.' I had a look and it was. Then the bed. 'It's for someone to dive in and pull the blankets back, so there must be a pull-switch.' I looked up the wall and pulled a door forward slightly. There was a litre bottle full of black powder in the wall with a detonator in the top where the cork should be. I left the door, walked out and asked the others for their toggle ropes. Getting as many as possible, I tied them together and went back in. I found one of the booby-trap leads and without touching it, put one of the ropes around it. Coming back outside, I started pulling it in. Then I got resistance. WHOOOFF! The bloody lot went up in the air.

A mile to the east, directly along the road was the River Dives and the Varaville Bridge which was thought to have been destroyed on

D-Day, but no one knew if this had been done successfully, and so a Recce Patrol was required to find out.[21]

That night, Keith Ponsford went off with a sergeant. They got a good way up the road, past some houses on the left and a large house on the right. A tree had been felled across the road so Ponsford said to the sergeant, 'It's not worth both of us going any further.' Beside the road was a big flooded ditch, so he stripped off, left his clothes with the sergeant and slipped into the water. He swam along the ditch to the bank of the bridge and saw that the structure was indeed still in one piece. Noting a solitary sentry, he started back. On the way he found some hides beside the road that contained Goliaths, wire-guided mini tanks full of explosives, and so did what he could to disable as many of them as possible. Consequently, the patrol took far longer than anticipated and on returning to his starting point, found that the sergeant, thinking that he was not coming back, had left and taken Ponsford's clothes with him. He got out of the water, removed some leeches and walked back down the road, starkers! I'm sure he said something rather nice to the sergeant when he got back.

The next morning, 18 August, 3 Troop was briefed to go and capture the bridge. The whole area was under water, having been flooded by the Germans before D-Day, so we had to do it on our flat feet, in daylight, down the long, straight road. Badger Hanson, a Royal Artillery bombardier, Ronny Bridges and myself got as far as the big house on the right. In a garage beside it, a hole had been made in the wall, obviously a position that the Paras had used on D-Day because we could see straight down the hedgerow to the bridge. It was an opportune moment because approaching behind it was a German section that thought they were out of sight. Badger said, 'Wait,' then 'Fire!' We all opened up, Hanson with a magazine of Thompson, Bridges giving rapid fire with his rifle, and me a magazine of .303. It was all over in seconds. No more Germans.

Our other Section had come up the left-hand side of the road and got to the houses, carried out a quick search and started moving forward. Then one of the Goliaths started clattering down the road.

[21] By the 1st Canadian Parachute Battalion and engineers of 3 Para Squadron. It was reported as destroyed. Bullshit. The bridge they destroyed was another one at Varaville that crossed the Divette.

There were shouts of 'Armour!' and everybody disappeared, except for Johnny Hawkesworth, a Guardsman, who walked into the middle of the road, picked up a block of wood, rested on it and started firing at this bloody thing coming down the road with 150 lb of explosive on it! He was trying to detonate it but the bullets were just bouncing off, yet for some reason it did spin around and stop. The lads looked at it for a while and Lieutenant Thompson decided that it had run over its own cable and there was no longer any control, and therefore could not be detonated. Moving up the side of the road, he took the Section past it and just as they got to the tree across the road, the Germans opened up. With wood and bark flying about, the Section crossed behind it and into the waterlogged ditch. Then came our turn to move. There was no cover at all in front, so our only option was to copy the other Section. We therefore ran up the left-hand side of the road, past the derelict Goliath to the tree trunk, then back across the road and into the ditch. The Germans fired at us all the way across the road and there must have been more lead than wood in that tree when they finished! Badger and myself moved into the fields to the right and there was a sudden explosion. A tank that had not been seen had begun firing from the other side of the river, and we were caught in the open. Big clods of earth were flying all over the shop and I thought, 'This is it', but the shells kept whizzing over our heads and we realized the gun could not be depressed enough. Badger immediately said, 'Get forward,' as the closer we got to the tank, the safer we were. The only problem was I couldn't move. I'd lost my 'north' and was paralysed, but Badger kicked me up the arse with a bloody good boot. Wallop! 'MOVE!' I did. It was just what was required to shake me out of it and after that I was all right. Reaching the others we began walking along the flooded ditch which was overhung with grass and weeds. On hearing a shell coming over, Cossey, the radio operator, with the '18' set on his back, went under the water. All you could see was the aerial, just like a periscope on a submarine.

We moved right up to the bridge and most people occupied an 'L' shaped slit trench. Facing us on the other side was infantry, a 20 mm Flak gun and the tank, although at that moment, it couldn't get us unless with its MG. Thompson decided that we had got to get across the river and picking out Hugh Melville, 'Ossie' Osbourne, Ted Pritchard and myself said, 'With me'. We slithered out of the trench like worms, up and over the bank into the river, swam across and then up the bank on the other side. We must have been seen because a Jerry opened fire and hit Melville. Ossie shot the German and Thommo ordered us back across the river, bringing Melville with us. We got back into the trench and put our emergency dressings on him but it was futile. Dickie Hughes got some fags out and we all sat there having a smoke. Eventually, Thommo said, 'We'll have to go back across,' so again it was back in the water and up the bank on the other side. There was a building lengthways on to us and a hedgerow in front with another building. We got into a barn on the left-hand side and worked our way forward. The end wall of the barn was made of wattle, a sort of wood covered with mud. There were big holes in it and we were looking through them at the German position along the hedgerow. The Flak gun was one of the four-barrelled types. I was fascinated by it, but thought, 'By Christ, if he opens up on us, goodnight nurse!' A soldier was standing beside it doing a search with binoculars. Suddenly, the binoculars came around to the end of the barn. I don't know what he thought he was going to find, but must have seen something through the barn wall, because he pointed towards us and screamed out. Well, we were gone, straight out the other end of the barn! The gun came round, fired and the end of the building just disappeared. We got back across the river.

By this time Ponsford had come up, and it was definite, we had to storm that bridge. It was essential for transport. We were thinking, 'We've got no support weapons here, no mortars, so it's going to be a straight old fashioned charge with small arms and grenades.' Thommo was going to lead it. On the signal, it had to be up, onto the road and then spread out as we ran. Everybody waited. 'Ready? One, two, GO!' The Troop was up and charging down the road. We got to within fifty yards of the bridge when there was an almighty explosion. The bridge went up in front of us in a thousand pieces. Everybody just dived to the ground as great lumps of stone came crashing down. As at Amfreville, if Jerry had waited fifteen seconds, he could have got the lot of us. No more 3 Troop. Back into the slit trench we went.

A little later the order came, 'Someone has got to go back across the river, they've blown the bridge, so they're probably pulling back.' We had to go and find out. Seven of us went back into the water, amongst all of the wreckage, up the bank and found that the Germans were still there! And so we had to get back yet again! Then the 20 mm Flak gun started up. I was lying on the bank, Thompson beside me, Ellis Norris with a Bren gun. Thommo said, 'We'll get across one at a time. When I say go, you go!' He went to poke his head above the bank and have a look, and I had the pleasure of sticking an officer's face in the mud! He spluttered and coughed, but I said, 'Sorry Sir, but don't stick your nut up like that! That's all they're looking for.' The first bloke went into the water, crossed to the other side and as he went up the bank, the Germans fired but missed. Next one. Across, and again the enemy missed him, but the bank at that point was getting more and more slippery. Thompson said, 'Away you go, Scotty.' I slid into the water, did a couple of strokes and was over. I began to move up the bank but to my horror started slipping on the mud. It felt like a nightmare where you were running forward but going backwards. I could hear the sound of firing but got over OK. Then Thommo risked it and made it. The bloke on that gun must have been very slow because he should have got one of us. Ellis Norris and the other two were caught over there as it became impossible to cross. They shouted something about trying to cross further down. We thought they'd had it.

A thick smoke screen was laid down that allowed us to move back, and walking along the road to Varaville, I saw Bungy Young who said, 'Scott. You're wounded.' 'Sir?' He pointed to my knee and I realized that my trousers were torn and my left knee was bleeding. A lump of flesh was missing from the inside of the leg, just above the kneecap, but I was lucky that whatever it was did not go in. I hadn't even felt it. Cold water, hot blood? After a bit of first aid it was back to duty.

The following morning, Ellis Norris and the two others turned up. They had found another spot further along the bank and were about to cross when one of them said he couldn't swim! Ellis asked him what he was doing in the Commandos and the bloke said, 'I'm not a Commando. I was in a Beach Group and got called up after D-Day.' So they had their weapons, a Bren gun and a non-swimmer. Ellis said to the other Commando, 'Throw his rifle across the river. Keep your rifle and strip the Bren down.' This was done and he then hurled the Bren's barrel, body and bipod across, but kept hold of the piston group. Then he took the other rifle and holding one end gave the other to the Commando and got into the water with the non-swimmer between them, resting on the rifle. They reached the other side, found the rifle and pieces of the Bren, assembled them and made their way back. Ponsford spoke to this poor soul from the Beach Group and then went to see Bungy, who said, 'It's not fair on the man and it's not fair on the people working with him because he doesn't know the way we work. We either find him a job within the Commando until he can go and get trained or we bin him out now. If we bin him now, where is he going to go?' So Bungy put him with Ned Moore in the Medical Section.

The next day we crossed the River Dives via a bridge to the south, heading towards a place called Dozule. The Troop was walking up a main road, with our Section leading. I had the Bren gun resting quite comfortably on my pack. Everybody was quite happy because we had all got away with it, surviving the previous day's actions. We turned left and there was a short hedge, then a driveway to a big house. Halfway across the drive we looked down it. Synnott and all those in front said the same thing, 'Oh my God!' Sitting along the drive was a mass of field grey! Some were cleaning weapons, others were eating, one was walking down the path with a box of grenades and they were all in different states of undress. We realized that it was the same men that had been at the bridge and they thought they were safe. Well, as quickly as people had looked and seen, we were charging down the drive. Everybody piled in there, following us. It was all over immediately, the Germans couldn't do a thing about it. Hands up, march out, that was that.[22]

*   *   *

The breakout continued and the Troop had to perform a liaison patrol to confirm that the 13th Parachute Battalion was on Dozule Hill. Finding that they were indeed in position we came back down the hill, rejoined the Commando and started on a night march. This was in single file along a railway line and then following white tape laid by guides, which saved those following up from having to do their own navigation. The last person was supposed to pick it up. The tape led to the heights at Angouville or 'Bully Beef Hill' as it became known.

[22] The Flak gun went to Christ Hospital, Petworth.

Each Troop branched off towards an objective. It was dead quiet except for the occasional thump of guns, but they were not troubling us and 3 Troop moved east, across country to a second class road going up the hill. Approaching a farm to our right one dozy German sentry was spotted outside the gate. He was taken care of and a party went into the farm while the other Section continued up the hill, took up positions around an ammunition bunker and waited. Two horse-drawn enemy carts then came over the hill and were promptly shot up by our Brens on the road. This woke the Jerries in the farm, who found a number of black-faced 3 Troop men in charge of their weapons, so it was the POW cage for them.

The morning wore on and at about 1100 hours a Kubelwagen suddenly drove straight up to the bunker to pick up some ammunition. About fifteen blokes fired at it from different positions but they must have been so surprised that only one man was hit and the remainder managed to run away. Shortly after, Jerry put in a very low-key attack up the hill but when engaged, just broke and ran. This was the end of the episode except for the arrival of the Quartermaster, Captain 'Slinger' Martin, who under cover of a smoke screen laid down by our guns, dashed up to us with jeeps full of ammunition and food. Then he took away the casualties, all under shell and mortar fire. Very exciting to watch!

A liaison patrol was required to go and link up with the 12th Parachute Battalion. A mate of mine, Smithy, was a signaller in their HQ, so I volunteered. There was no Jerry about, 12 Para had seen to that. I found Smithy in a house in a home-made shelter, comprising two upright pianos and a third as a roof. Bomb proof! They were all drinking and smoking vile smelling cigars. I asked, 'Where did you get those?' 'We captured a German officer's mess lorry!' I was taken back down the hill to 3 Commando at speed, on a trailer behind a jeep, the bumpiest ride I have ever experienced.

Then it was off to Pont L'Eveque. Another night infiltration, all across country, everyone cheesed off, bloody tired and itchy. We plodded on and entered the village. Not a sausage. We were allocated an area to dig in and my position was by the road outside a farm. I dug a nice hole and lined it with straw. Head cover was some concrete fence posts. Lovely! I installed the gun and had just got some grub ready when the order came, 'Prepare to move!' So there was no knife and fork etiquette, it was racing spoon time. Gulp it down!

Moving east towards a place called Beuzeville, we were told that the Brigade was being withdrawn from action and were duly shifted north, finishing up in an orchard beside a little lane leading to Honfleur. Everyone was sitting around and as far as we were concerned it was all over. People were having a fag, cleaning up and then there was an accident. One of our officers had found a German Verey light pistol, and I am pleased to say he was not a 3 Troop officer. The first thing to do when you picked up any weapon was to check that it was safe. This officer hadn't and was walking through the orchard twiddling it round his finger like John Wayne. When he got hold of it he accidentally pulled the trigger and the flare shot out, hitting a bloke straight in the midriff. The medics could not do a thing for him. What a way to finish up, all because of a piece of stupidity.

Then more bad news. Some Polish armour at the bottom of the road had been into Honfleur and said it was clear of Germans, but as tanks could not check everything, a foot patrol was required to go in there. Of course, 3 Commando got the job, 3 Troop got the job, our Section got the job. Jimmy Synnott said, 'All we've got to do is walk down the road, have a peep in Honfleur and come back. Dead easy. Shouldn't take too long, couple of hours and it'll all be over,' and off we went. On the way, we heard armour approaching and so got into ambush positions, but it turned out to be a Polish Sherman. We shouted at them and they stopped. The Poles could only understand the odd word of English and were saying, 'OK, OK, nix Allemagne, kein Deutsch!' Our response was, 'You were bloody lucky!' We carried on into Honfleur and to say we were off-guard, well, we might as well have been going to the bloody cinema. The road opened out into a square and there was a wall on the right hand side. On this wall was a pissoir. We came round a corner and found ourselves on the quayside. Sitting down along the quay amongst all the fishing nets was an 88 mm gun and its crew. The next thing I knew, Ryder, our medic, was looking at me. I'd been blown well away from where I had been standing. Someone said, 'He's dead.' Ryder said, 'No he isn't,' and I passed out. When I came round, they had strapped me to a stretcher and I was being loaded onto the back of an Airborne jeep; I could see the red beret of the driver. I passed out again.

When I came around, the jeep was travelling across country. Next I recall being carried into a big red brick-fronted house and then lying on a bed. I looked to my right – Germans. Looked straight ahead – Germans! My immediate thought was, 'The bleedin' driver's taken the wrong road.' Then there was a German officer standing by my bed, and his first words, in English, were, 'You are in a German Field Hospital.' I thought, 'I know what's coming now.' But then he said, 'We have been taken over by the British and you will be evacuated.' 'Thank Christ for that!' We were in Beuzeville. Shortly after, an old Austin ambulance turned up and they hauled me in there. A few other British wounded joined me and I think I was in the best condition, as they had all lost limbs and were battered about. I was complete but useless, couldn't move anything. I could see and hear but that was it, the proverbial sack of spuds. We finished up in a big, tented hospital in Bayeux.

I stayed in this hospital for what seemed like ages without making any progress until a group of doctors came in and one said, 'We're going to try something.' They turned me on my side. 'We're going to put a probe into your spine to check for a reaction.' What I didn't know was while they were telling me, it had already been done. I just lay there. They started a mumbled discussion and came back. 'Well, we didn't have much success with that one. We'll try another one.' And once again, they had already done it. No reaction. Back to the bottom of the bed they went, more mumbling and then, 'We're going to try a third.' This time I nearly flew off the bed! Apparently, they had inserted it a few inches higher up my back and now knew what they wanted to know. They got to work on me and after about two further weeks I had virtually returned to normal.

The ward was mixed, so to speak. The bloke in the bed next to me was a German Para (who I taught to play Ludo) and the two end beds contained Hitler Youths from the 12th SS Panzer Division. I knew I was on the road to recovery when one of them swore at the Matron, 'Schweine Engländer.' I thought, 'No. I'm not having that.' So I went down there and grabbed him by the hair and the balls and gave him a bouncing on the bed. It took five orderlies to drag me off! In the morning I had to go and see the Hospital Commandant who said, 'I'm not going to have anybody treating my patients like that.' 'But he was swearing at the Matron.' He said, 'That's another story.

105

If you're fit enough to do that, you're fit enough to get out of this hospital,' and he bounced me out!

I was sent to a transit camp which was situated alongside a road about a mile outside Arromanches. I fell in with some wounded Paras and a bloke out of 6 Commando. In the morning on parade, we went through the British Army muster. A sergeant-major said, 'All the infantry over there, all the artillery and corps men over there.' We just stood on our own and he did his nut. 'I said all infantry over there!' We replied, 'We're not infantry, we're specialist troops.' He would not have it, so in the end he said, 'You, you, you and you, go to the cookhouse.' We did a smart turn to the right and headed back to the tents. Sod him. We went through this every morning, and in the end he realized it was no good, though he still used to say, 'You, you, you and you ...!'

By now, I knew that the 1st Special Service Brigade had returned to England. One day, the bloke from 6 Commando and myself went for a walk down to the beach at Arromanches, the site of the Mulberry harbour, and saw six very distinguished looking jeeps. They had Vickers 'K' guns and Browning .50s mounted. I said to him, 'I bet that is No. 2 Sabre Squadron, SAS. No one else in the British Army has jeeps like that.' I walked up to the number four jeep where a bloke lay stretched out on top of the dunnage and said, 'Oi mate.' He sat up. 'Yes?' 'Are you Sabre Squadron of the SAS?' 'Yes. How do you know?' 'By your jeeps. The only other mob that use Vickers K's is us.' He asked what our units were, and then I said, 'You're not going back to Blighty by any chance? We're trying to get back, but we're stuck in the transit camp up the road.' He said, 'Yes. I'll tell you what. We're embarking in about half an hour. If you can get back to the transit camp and get your kit, I'll take you on the LST. What you do when you get to England is up to you.' So we slogged it back to the transit camp, jumped in the tent, grabbed our gear and stuffed it all in one bag. The Para boys were saying, 'What's going on?' I just shouted to them about what had happened while I continued to pack. We knew we were not going to make it back because there was not enough time, the distance was too great and we were not fit enough to run it, but were going to have a go anyway. We belted towards the camp gate and got to the Guard Room, thinking they are bound to come out and ask where we are going. Traffic of course was on the right, but bloody Englishmen, they stick to their own ideas. As we got there, a 15 cwt Bedford pulled in on the left-hand side of the road. Why? Because it was easier for the driver to get out. Leaving the engine running, he got down from the cab and went across the road to report in at the Guard Room. He must have started nattering to them, so I said to my mate, 'Quick, jump in!' He dived in one side, I dived behind the wheel and we were gone! I drove down the road to Arromanches and straight onto the beach, pulling up beside the jeeps. The SAS bloke said, 'You made it!' I said, 'Well I had to nick this!' 'Right, well jump on, make yourself comfortable.' We moved along one of the Mulberry Harbour quays and onto the LST. The man who had helped us was none other than Roy Farran.[23]

[23] Roy Farran is an SAS legend. I believe he was the founder member of L detachment, later SAS, and took part in multiple operations in the Desert, Italy and North-West Europe, plus Palestine in 1947. For further information read his book, *Winged Dagger* (Collins, 1948).

Chapter 10

Back in Blighty

The LST arrived in Southampton and we disembarked. One of Roy Farran's people found that there was a money exchange office and as they all had Lire, Francs and Marks, went over to change it. When asked if we were going to change ours, I said, 'We ain't got any money!' The next thing we knew they had had a whip round and gave us a pile of different currencies. The next stroke of luck was that the parents of my 6 Commando friend actually lived in Southampton, so we went over to their house. Unfortunately, no one was in, but at least there was something to eat. What to do next? I knew that 3 Commando would be at the Commando Group HQ in Petworth, West Sussex, and once there, my friend could find out where 6 Commando was. We hitch-hiked our way, found the camp and walked into the Orderly Room situated in a Nissen hut. The sergeant there, Henderson, took one look at me and said, 'You're dead!' I said, 'No I ain't!' They had received a report stating that I had been killed, so I went through what had happened.[24]

All of the lads were on leave, so he put me in one of the 3 Troop Nissen huts and all I had to do was hang around until they came back, which wasn't very long. They started drifting back in ones and twos, and everyone made the same remark as they entered the hut. 'What are you doing here? You're dead!'

I was given some leave and went home. While there a telegram arrived instructing me not to return to Petworth, but to report back to Worthing instead. I therefore took up my billet with Mrs Ford

[24] My mother never received a telegram on this occasion and I have never been able to find out why.

again. That first night back in the Ham Hotel, people were asking, 'Has so-and-so come back with you? What happened to him?' This did not make for a good evening.

Since 3 Commando had arrived home, Peter Young had been promoted to be deputy commander of No. 3 Commando Brigade in Burma. Lieutenant Colonel Komrower had taken over as CO of 3 Commando.

During this period when we were getting back up to strength, Ned Moore issued a request for people, possibly with first aid training, to help at Worthing hospital, which was short staffed. I went to see Ned Moore and then reported to the hospital. While there, our duties were split. For a couple of days we would be in the operating theatre in white coats and masks, wheeling the patients in and sterilizing instruments. Other days were spent helping the orderlies in the wards or in the Treatment Room where they were bandaging people. One morning I was asked to remove the stitches of a little boy of about ten years of age who had been operated on for appendicitis. I asked for some scissors to snip the stitches and tweezers to pull them out but was told they wouldn't be needed because the 'stitches' were clips, a new idea, and a nurse showed me what to do. Once removed, they left a small ridge of skin that went down after a few days, leaving a clean scar. I went down to the ward, found the boy and told him what I was going to do. To badger him up I said, 'Do you want to keep them as a souvenir?' He didn't want them, but then looked at me, noticed my Army trousers and said, 'Are you one of them Commandos?' I said, 'Yeah.' He said, 'Cor, you wait 'til I get back to school and tell them I had my stitches taken out by a Commando!'

Obviously a lot of the patients were military and once, in the operating theatre, I had to treat a mate of mine, Johnny Coates, who had a lot of shrapnel in the calf. I took him into the X-Ray Room, put on big gloves and held a panel over his leg while the doctor located the pieces of shrapnel. In each place where there was a piece of iron he inserted a needle to mark the position with some sort of dye. It was amazing that Johnny didn't feel a thing. He was then taken to surgery to have all the pieces removed.

On another day, in the Treatment Room a bloke with impetigo came in and gave me his slip from the Doctor. I said, 'Do you know what the Doctor's put on this?' He said, 'No.' 'I've got to take all those scabs off and when I do, the sores are going to start running. The Doctor's put that the quickest way to dry them out is surgical spirit.' He just said, 'OK.' 'Are you sure? When I do it, it's going to sting.' 'Oh that's all right if it stings a bit.' 'It won't sting a bit, IT STINGS!' He still wasn't fussed, so I started shaving his face. Then I got a tray with the necessary swabs and spirit and asked him if he was ready. 'Yeah.' 'You'd better get hold of the arms of that chair and hold on tight.' I started dabbing and he went straight up in the air! These were the kind of things we had to do.

Due to working in the hospital we were some of the first people to know that there was trouble in Belgium. One night we were told to report to the hospital. Single-decker buses had been converted to ambulances with stretcher beds and these came in from Shoreham aerodrome, full of Yanks. To put it mildly, they were all in crap order. The Doctor came on the buses with us, looking at the labels and telling us where to put the wounded. I asked one who had a crushed leg, how it had happened. He said, 'I was trying to get out of the position and fell over, right in front of this bloody tank, one of our own, and it ran straight over my leg.' He had to go immediately to the operating theatre to have it cut off. The amputated mess of a leg was given to an orderly, me, to incinerate. The task was carried out and I returned to the operating theatre via the kitchens, where a strong black coffee was enjoyed en route.

* * *

Some of 3 Troop had got early leave, and I was in the second batch ready to go. They had left saying, 'You're the lucky ones, you're going to be home for Christmas,' but we now knew that the 6th Airborne Division was on its way out to the Ardennes, and as the Brigade was loosely attached, it was obvious that it would not be long before we joined them. Sure enough, during one of the following nights, I heard a vehicle pull up outside the billet. I got up, opened the window and saw that it was a Commando jeep. 'What's up?' 'Everybody has got to get themselves down to the station by 0230 hours.' The station was half a mile away. I had thirty minutes to dress, gather my kit and Bren gun and run down there.

Chapter 11

North-West Europe

By the appointed time, everybody was at Worthing Station. Two blokes had turned up drunk, which would not have been a problem, but they also arrived without their kit. They were immediately booted out, their green berets taken away. We travelled to Gravesend, boarded *The Lady of Mann* to Ostend, and finished up in the snow and ice of the Ardennes Forrest. The weather was like the Russian Front and we had no overcoats or gloves, but wore leather jerkins under our Para smocks, and these were very good for keeping out the chill of the wind. Some cut up their army blankets and sewed them into the smock as an extra lining. Anyway, when you're frozen you don't feel the cold.

As usual, the Brigade was split up and No. 3 Commando went with the American 9th Army. This was for Operation *Blackcock*, our job being to clear the last triangle of resistance on the northern side of what had been 'The Bulge'. We were working with the 7th Armoured Division and 1/5th Queen's. *Blackcock* started rolling in the region of Sittard, then moved on to Maeseyck. We stayed in a convent and some of our blokes actually got the nuns to do their washing for them! Commandos were very persuasive, charming ... While there, during the night we heard a scuffle outside and saw the Field Military Police arresting three Americans. The next day it was found that they were in fact three Germans dressed in American uniform.

From there it was a few miles further east to Stevensweert where we found a glass coffin that had been smashed. The occupant had been an old bishop who had until then been preserved, but had now turned to dust. Moving on through nearby Eiland, we crossed the

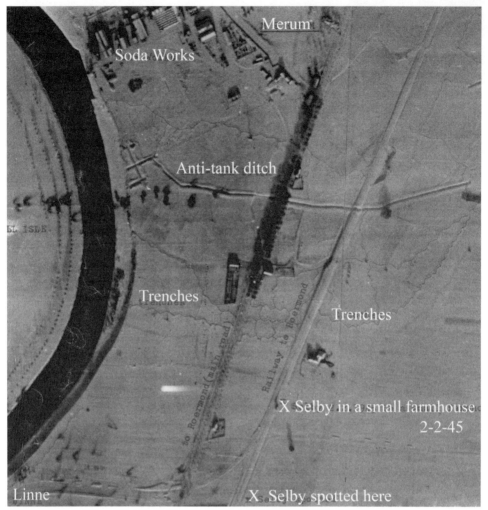

Linne.

frozen Juliana Canal, some walking over the ice itself, to Maasbracht and finished up just west of the town of Linne on the River Maas. The Troop advanced over the Montforterbeek, turned left towards a Chateau, along an embankment and into a deep Jerry trench. Jimmy Synnott noticed that there was some dead ground in front and said, 'Scotty, take your Bren and go out there as a forward alarm post. I'll send a relief in an hour or so.' At about 2200 hours I took up position on the lip of the hollow, shovelled the snow away to get out of the wind, lay down and waited. There was no grief, flares were going up, a few shells whizzing over, mortar crumps and the occasional shot, but not at us. The only trouble was I wanted to go to sleep, but you had to keep yourself awake. Time passed. I needed to relieve myself, but held on for an age until I just had to roll over and kneel up for a pee. After quite a while I began to think, 'Where's that sentry relief?' At first light I was still waiting, so I thought, 'It's an exposed position, move back.' I arrived back in the trench to find 5 Troop there. 'Where's 3 Troop?' 'Gone for a hot meal and a couple of hours kip.' 'Where?' 'In that barn by the road.' Over I go and found Jimmy Synnott, who immediately apologized. He had been so pleased to be relieved that he had completely forgotten about sending me out in front. I then tried to get a hot drink. 'Too late, Scotty. We are moving out to attack Linne.'

This attack was carried out Russian style, with 3 Commando, less 3 Troop, charging across the frozen plain and crashing into Linne on the backs of tanks. 3 Troop was tasked with a left hook, on foot, to the river and church to try and cut off any enemy leaving that side of town. We duly followed the route, but most of the Germans had already retreated to the other side of the river.

After the street fighting and house clearing, the town was burning and we were ordered to put the fires out! We couldn't. The water was frozen and consequently the houses just burned themselves out.

Afterwards, Troop HQ, plus myself as Bren gunner, took up position in a cellar of a house on a road junction on the Linne–Roermond road. Another Section occupied an isolated house opposite. Dickie Hughes' Section was positioned in another house a little further along the Roermond road.

There was nothing in Linne. During their retreat the Germans had taken anything they could carry. This included every door, mattress, anything that could be used, and what they couldn't take they smashed. However, I had a real good look around and managed to make the cellar quite comfortable. I found the ash tray base of a fire in one place, the middle section in another, the flue somewhere else and a pipe going out onto the road above. Wood was used from wrecked houses to get it going nicely. I had straw to line the floor and any holes were plugged with anything else available.

Having been there a few days, on 2 February news arrived about an incident involving Walter Selby, my friend who had followed me from the Maidstone Infantry Training Centre. He and a bloke called

Connolly had gone out on a jeep and taken a wrong turning on the way back. They ran into some barbed wire and while Selby was reversing the jeep, drove over a mine, writing off the vehicle. As per training, the two of them had moved in separate directions to make their way back to the Commando positions. Connolly had returned injury-free, but Selby was missing presumed dead.

A German Minnewerfer situated in a factory at Merum, two miles to the north, began to open up at certain times of the day, six bombs at a time. It started at one end of town and moved across. Between firing and reloading for the next salvo there was about a twenty-minute gap. Another of my old friends, Don Harding, went out in a jeep with an Artillery OP group and on the way back into town was travelling along the road opposite my junction. The 'Minnie Werfer' (as we called them) opened up and a bomb landed right behind the jeep. He dived into a slit trench alongside the road and another bomb then fell straight in the bloody trench. Thankfully, he wouldn't have known a thing about it.

These Minnie Werfers could also fire oil bombs which on impact would burst into flame. One of them landed beside my house but failed to ignite, and just splattered the wall with black tar instead.

A sergeant replacement, 'Shiny boots' Cassidy, arrived at the house and asked, 'Where's my room?' I said, 'Well, I've made myself comfortable down here in the cellar.' He said, 'I'm not sleeping down there.' I replied, 'It's up to you, but I wouldn't sleep up there.' Nevertheless, he stayed upstairs because there was a bed. I just thought, 'You won't be there long mate!' During the evening the time arrived and the shrieking of the Minnie Werfer duly started. There came a voice came from above. 'What is that?' 'It's a Moaning Minnie, fires six bombs at a time. Starts off at this time every night. Sometimes it begins at this side of the town, sometimes the other . . .' It didn't take him long to come down those bloody steps!

During the morning of 5 February, I paid a visit to the house occupied by Dickie Hughes' Section. When I got there, most people were tired and I don't know why but I offered to do a STAG for them. So up I went to the attic. It was pretty comfortable, with a chair to sit on, and a set of binoculars along with a sniper's rifle and telescopic sight. There was quite a stretch of country to cover, all nice and white because of the snow. After a while I saw movement. As per training I looked away and then turned back. There was movement again, so picked up the binoculars, and zoned in on a person crawling in the snow about 600 yards away. Every now and then he stopped, lifted his head and looked around. Then he carried on crawling. I thought it was a German sniper trying to get into position, so I picked up the rifle, zoned the sight in and readied myself. 'The next time you put your head up mate, I'm going to put a bullet in it.' I was ready with the first pressure taken on the trigger. He lifted his head up and I recognized him instantly. It was Selby. I had almost shot my own mate. I couldn't recognize him with the binoculars, but through the sniper's sight he was nice and clear. I set the rifle down, put the safety catch on, called up Dickie Hughes and told him what I'd seen. He said, 'You've got to be joking Scotty, he's been out there for three nights. No one could survive out there for that long.' I insisted it was Selby, so a report went through to Commando Headquarters and Captain Pollard came forward with a patrol from 6 Troop to go out and get him. While they were assembling in the courtyard at the bottom of our house, a jeep driven by 'Tankie' Thompson turned up with Ned Moore. They said, 'What's all this about Selby? The next thing we knew they had driven out there. I went back upstairs and watched. They tore up the road towards Selby, picked him up, bunged him on a stretcher, strapped him on the jeep and came back in reverse, all the way to the village. I went downstairs and had a quick look at him. His leg was shattered. The jeep's accelerator is a flat elongated piece of metal and when the mine went off, it had been forced right up between his tibia and fibia. To all intents and purposes he had been a goner, but had crawled, eating handfuls of snow for water, found shelter in a chicken coop and had just about survived. He was immediately evacuated.[25]

At this stage the Brigade gained some artillery support in the shape of the 1st Mountain Regiment, RA. Mountain Artillery! Typically, the British Army had posted them to Holland! They possessed short-range, 75 mm howitzers that could be dismantled, moved and

---

[25] The 3 Commando war diary is wrong. It states that Captain Pollard was recommended for a VC for rescuing Selby, when the patrol did not get a chance to go out and get him. I met Selby in 2002 in Heidelberg (he lived in Baden Baden) and he still didn't know what had happened to him. When I told him he said, 'Yes, I knew it was the Doctor.'

reassembled. The unit had been stagnating through lack of use and had found their way to the Hook of Holland to be shipped back to England. Brigadier Mills-Roberts had gone there for something, came across them, thought they could be of use and had them attached to the Brigade. They were extremely effective and came in very handy. In one action, with the guns being howitzers they could not get an angle onto a particular target that was proving to be a problem. However, they had an idea. One was taken to pieces, carried to the top of a block of flats, reassembled, and the target knocked out. The gun was then dismantled and taken back down. Problem solved.

3 Commando was relieved in Linne by 46 Royal Marines Commando. We moved to Montfort to take over from US troops. Arriving in the dead of night, Jimmy Synnott led us into the Yank position. There was one White half-track with a sentry asleep inside it. In the house there were six more asleep. Jimmy kicked the nearest sleeping bag and woke what turned out to be a sergeant, who rose, grabbed his carbine and wrapped it in his sleeping bag. He then woke the others who, half asleep, did exactly the same thing! Out they went and making enough noise to wake Berlin, started up the half-track and scarpered. Some handover.

The next morning, we did a recce of the village and found a US Mobile Canteen in the square. It provided such things as doughnuts, coffee, chewing gum and Lucky Strike cigarettes. Three women were serving and Jimmy Synnott asked, 'What are you doing here?' They said, 'We are here for the American boys.' Informing them that the Yanks had gone, and obviously not being there for the benefit of British troops, they decided to leave. However, Jimmy said, 'You won't be able to drive out of the village because Jerry is watching the road and will blast this thing sky high.' So they abandoned the wagon and left anyway. Of course 3 Troop had a birthday.

Operation *Blackcock* finished in late February. We had crossed the River Meuse without too much problem and then training began for the crossing of the River Rhine, although all we really did was embarkation and disembarkation drills from amphibious troop carriers called Buffaloes. Our objective was the important communications town of Wesel.

The operation was set for the night of 23/24 March and I must have been the happiest man on the crossing that night. It had been my turn to collect the rum ration for the lads, so I had six rations in my mess tin. However, when I got back, no one wanted it. I couldn't just throw it away and so said, 'What shall I do with it?' The response was, 'You drink it!' 'What, all of it?' Of course the comments came back about my not being 'up to it'. Being young and having my machismo questioned, I drank it.

Then came the crossing, made under a very heavy barrage of all calibres. Light anti-aircraft guns fired tracer rounds to mark the boundaries of the crossing points. Some of the men were in Schnell boats, an open craft with a motor at the back, but the majority used Buffaloes. Our Buffalo had easily crossed a number of dykes on the way, but when we got to the Rhine the angle of the bank sent the nose deep into the water, right up to the shield. However, before the water could swamp us, the vehicle bobbed back up and levelled out. Under fire from a German artillery barrage, the vehicles started crossing, but the strong current forced us down river. An artillery officer, Major O'Flaherty, ex-3 Commando, spotted that our own barrage was not moving forward and that we would run into it if it was not lifted, plus Jerry was jamming the radio signals. Using his initiative, O'Flaherty moved the barrage forward, away from us. My Buffalo reached the east side, stuck its nose up the bank and I jumped out, but being drunk, nearly fell back into the Rhine. I made my way up the bank and jumped into a trench, straight onto the stomach of a dead German whose body let out a large burp. Bingo – I was sober immediately. The Brigade then carried on towards Wesel and waited on the outskirts while the RAF bombed it. The advance resumed almost before the raid had finished and the night was spent mopping up pockets of resistance.

* * *

During the morning we were consolidating our positions and I was on watch at the top of a wrecked block of flats. In front of me was a large open area, with tramlines in the middle. Half-right was a gap in the ruins and through there I could see a green space, perhaps a park. I was bored. Suddenly, a movement to the right caught my eye. I had another look. It was five German Paras coming down the edge of the open space. One of them began to move ahead in bounds, down, up, dash. I aimed for a telephone pole in his path, about 300 yards away. He gradually approached the pole and as he went behind it I squeezed the trigger. He came out the other side and met the bullet, straight through the neck. Down he went. At that distance, a good shot. I even missed his chinstrap! Up came Jimmy Synnott. 'What's up?' 'A German, I just shot him. He was over there with four of his mates.' He said, 'Why didn't you wait for the others? We could have got the bloody lot of them!' And he started having a go at me. I said, 'Oh for Christ's sake Jimmy,' although I did deserve a bollocking and was getting one! Suddenly we began to hear a great murmuring roar. Looking west, we could see the staggering spectacle of the approaching 17th US and 6th British Airborne Divisions who were to land a few miles to the east of us. The scale of it stunned everyone, and my bollocking was forgotten.[26]

In the afternoon the Brigade was ordered to advance and link up with the US Airborne. 3 Commando left Wesel by road march and took up position in a farm. The first Airborne soldier we saw was an unarmed American who ran into our position and asked for chow and cigarettes! Thommo told him in no uncertain terms to go back to the DZ and find his rifle and equipment. Then it was a sixty-mile plod towards Munster. At a particular crossroads, some of our jeeps had come up and turned into a courtyard. Then armour of the American 'Hell on Wheels' Division and Churchills of the Irish Guards came up the road carrying Yank Paras. I was sitting on the bonnet of a jeep, minding my own business and happened to look up, only to see two aircraft coming down, seemingly without propellers. 'What are they for Christ's sake?' Then sparks began to come from them. 'Machine guns!' I dived under the jeep. There was a WHOOSH, followed by the rattle of machine gun fire and they were gone. It had taken all of fifteen seconds and they had shot up the whole junction. We found out later that they were Messerschmitt 262 jet fighters.

Beside this courtyard was a house, so I went over there for a scrounge, opened the back door and was faced by a set of stairs going up to the next floor. Lying across the stairs was a whole family. Four kids, the wife and husband, a soldier. He had shot them and then committed suicide. I got out as quickly as I could and told the Medical Section, not that they could do anything for them.

[26] We took about 850 POWs in Wesel.

We crossed the Dortmund–Ems Canal without any problem and headed for Greven. First into the town were elements of the 6th Airborne Division. We lodged ourselves in some houses along the main road and a mate and I decided to find something to eat. Passing through the backs of some houses we discovered one which had a full table laid! White cloth, plates, knives, forks and spoons. Then some orderlies brought in lunch, meat, veg and bread. It was obviously the Officer's Mess of some Airborne mob. So we 'borrowed' it. Scarpering back to the billet, the meal was shared with our mates. Needs must when you're hungry!

Leaving Greven was another night march, to Osnabrück, twenty miles away. Here the Paras were to hold onto the outskirts and 3 Commando would penetrate by the north-west, a hilly part of the town. Reaching this area we found a terminus point with a couple of wrecked, burning trams, opposite a small park and a pub. The road descended at a gradual slope until encountering a sharp bend, possibly a nice position for an enemy machine gun. Consequently, Jimmy Synnott decided that we would push a tram down the hill to cover us. At the point of daylight we started out with the tram, but unfortunately it began to pick up speed and rattled down the slope, leaving us behind. It came off the rails on the bend and crashed straight into the building we were concerned about. The danger point was passed at the double and we entered the still burning town. 3 Troop encountered little resistance. One POW was found in a block of flats, a Panzer driver with both arms badly burned, and his very nice wife. We left him there and his wife remained safe, if only for as long as we were there. On the top floor was a woman with a crying baby. The mother was terrified of us. She had no baby milk, so we collected our Compo dried milk, crushed some biscuits, mixed it up and fed it to the baby. She looked at us quite differently after that.

There was one stroppy old sod though who just wouldn't shut up. He kept calling me, 'Engländer schweinhund.' He lost his gold Hunter watch. Fair enough. If I were Russian I would have shot him.

A woman walking along the road was stopped and a .22 automatic pistol found in her bag. A member of the Werewolf Resistance? We didn't think so. The pistol was confiscated and she was given a kick up the arse and sent on her way.

121

Our stay in Osnabrück was short and we moved north-east towards the Weser, a deep, wide, moderate flowing river which we encountered between Stolzenau and Leese. The Rifle Brigade had met opposition here. Brigadier Mills-Roberts decided on a right flanking movement, across the river and go right, then swing left for Leese, all carried out during darkness. On the opposite bank the white tape system was to be employed.

During the night of 7/8 April the Brigade began crossing in flat-bottomed plywood, canvas-sided Goatley boats, propelled by the use of paddles. Reaching the opposite bank, 6 Commando led, laying the tape, then 46 and 45 RM Commandos and tail end Charlies, 3 Commando. 6, 45 and 46 went left to Leese while No. 3 peeled off right and attacked a V-Weapon factory in the woods. During this assault, while under fire, Colonel Bartholomew, who had taken over from Komrower, stood up on a tank, directed its gun onto targets and prompted the factory to give up. I didn't cross with 3 Troop, having been assigned to the rear party to bring up stores. My crossing was later, in daylight, and again by rowing across in a Goatley boat. I felt naked, under observation and waiting to get clobbered, but we got across without incident. The day was spent digging out deserters, old men of the *Volksturm*, and pacifying the locals who thought the Russians were coming.

We had now left the 6th Airborne Division and were attached to the 11th Armoured Division, the 'Raging Bull', yet there was no respite. It was now on towards Essel on the River Aller. Approaching it, we began to notice a decidedly awful smell.

The 1st Commando Brigade as we were now known, was faced with two bridges about a mile apart for the crossing of the Aller. 3 Commando was assigned a railway bridge on the left at Schwarmstadt, 6 Commando got the road bridge over to the right. We approached the railway bridge in the dark across open fields. The railway was on an embankment and the first stand of the bridge started over dry land. The Germans had tried to blow it, but their charges had either been badly or wrongly laid and they had failed. These stands had just fallen onto the ground, so 3 Troop led the way across on the girders, some men in stockinged feet in order not to make any noise. Unfortunately, due to carelessness or tiredness, two German sentries were allowed to run for it and we started chasing them! They should never have been in a position to run, and it was unfortunate that they were not caught and stuffed before getting the chance. 'Ossie' Osbourne and I, along with the rest of the Section, reached the embankment on the other side and could suddenly hear the, 'Crunch, crunch, crunch' of marching soldiers. Nice. A large column of Germans was coming along the road and they had no idea we were there, even though their sentries had been chased off the bridge. We couldn't believe it. That sort of thing just did not happen. As they got closer Ossie shouted, 'Halt! Hände hoch! Du bist gefangener!' The leading file of three men opened fire. We just let fly. Some ran for it, but for most, that was that.

Everybody moved along the embankment, entered a pine forest and after about a hundred yards took up position with our backs to the river. We dug in but had great trouble with all the tree roots. 3 Commando was holding the centre of the line, 45 and 46 Royal Marine Commandos were on the left and 6 Commando to our right. The Germans put in an effort that evening but it was the following morning that the whole Brigade endured fierce attacks. There was plenty of snap-shooting and LMG fire at close quarter, but grenades could not be thrown because of the density of the trees. All day the Germans just kept on bashing at us. They carried out the normal infantry tactic for such an environment. Starting with a line of skirmishers, they would advance in a straight line through the wood, as if they were beating game. When the firing started they got down, then support fire, including heavy machine guns, covered anyone who made a dash forward. At one stage the underbrush caught fire, although it was soon doused, but the smoke made it chaotic for both sides. About fifteen yards to my left a Bren gun team of McGonagal (a sniper of forty-nine kills) and Brown had a sharp shoot-out with a party of Jerry Marines, whom they killed. However, a subsequent MG burst killed McGonagal, who took it all in the head and shoulders, and severely wounded Les Brown. The Germans were fighting us tooth and nail. It got to a point where Jimmy Synnott said, 'What have you got left?' 'About half a magazine' (fourteen rounds). For a Bren gun that is nothing. He asked a few others and they were all short, so he, Spencer and a bloke called Ferrie went to get some ammo. Time went by and they did not return. Here we were with no Synnott, Spencer, Ferrie, Brown, McGonagal and a few others, and that was only from our Section. Then came the crisis. We could see the German Marine Battalion beginning to form up in front us for another attack from the edge of the wood. With so little ammunition we were in trouble. Suddenly, a tremendous barrage started up, with 25-pounders, 5.5- and 7.2-inch, all sorts of guns being fired. The shells passed overhead and plastered the leading edge of the wood. It was all over within minutes, leaving bodies, bits of bodies and busted, smoking, burning trees. Fortunately for us, the Forward Observation Officer of the Mountain Artillery had also seen the German activity. He did not have enough firepower to do much with his small Mountain guns and so had radioed the codename 'Shelldrake' for Commander, Royal Artillery, to request a Vector shoot. This meant that every gun within range of the stated target was to give it three rounds rapid fire.

If the Germans had managed to attack, we would have ended up using shovels and knives. Just after the barrage, Vickers guns opened up and in went 6 Commando. Their CO, Lewis, sounded the bugle horn and they charged across the open ground and through the woods in an attempt to capture the road bridge, an overall distance of about 500 yards. And they did it. Awesome! It was the last time that a bugle was sounded in the British Army for a bayonet charge.

We then had a brew and a smoke and awaited orders. Word arrived that Jimmy Synnott had not come back because as he, Jimmy Ferrie and Spencer had walked out of the wood to cross a road, they were all shot and wounded.

New orders did not take long in arriving. 'No. 1 Commando Brigade will advance in the direction, north-east of Luneburg, Uelzen, Bergen-Belsen.' We walked up a 'B' Class road, through a wood. Everyone had been commenting on the appalling smell and as we passed through this wood it was getting worse. We had smelt the stench from two miles away, and I am not saying a smell wafting on the breeze, I say a stench. It was almost physical. One felt unclean just to smell it. A message came through that there was a truce in that small area and there was to be no shooting. The road led to the back of Belsen Concentration Camp. German sentries were still standing at the bloody gate. There were dead bodies, walking skeletons with big bulging eyes staring at us. We had to just march past it. What could we do? All you got was a deep sense of disgust. After that, anything that was bloody German you knocked over.

A lot of good blokes were lost on the Aller, people who had come right through from Normandy and all because the Germans had fought so hard to try and stop us finding that camp.

It was then another move by both road march and transport to the north-east of Lüneburg. The Brigade now left the 11th Armoured Division and joined the 15th Scottish for the crossing of the last river, the Elbe. The 15th Scottish was a very good Division and we were quite happy with them, and I presume they with us.

The idea behind the Elbe crossing, set for the 27/28 April, was to capture Lauenburg, the road and rail bridges and link up with the US 9th Army. The river was very wide with a fast current. On our side were steep dykes, on the other 150-foot cliffs. The Brigade was again using Buffaloes with 6 Commando leading followed by 46 and 45 RM Commandos, then us. 6 Commando met a hail of grenades from the cliff tops but pressed on. 46 RM Commando carried on into Lauenburg and began clearing the town. 6 Commando captured the bridges intact, so on 29/30 April the 6th Airborne and 11th Armoured Divisions passed through on their way east. We then met up as planned with the Yanks of the 9th Army.

3 Troop were the first people into Lübeck. I found a tuppeny ha'penny camera that was easy to use and had a bit of film in it and so was taking a few photos without believing they would ever come out.[27]

The Brigade arrived at Wismar on the Baltic, and 3 Troop was sent on a patrol to the east of the town. Moving up the left-hand side of the road we saw these people coming down the right-hand side. We couldn't make them out because some were in long overcoats, others in part-German uniform. Seeing us, they got down into firing positions. Then a bloody great tank came round the corner behind them. With a bit of shouting it was realized that they were Russians and once happy that they knew who we were, moved forward, said, 'How do you do Russki,' sort of thing and shook hands. They were wearing all they had got. They seemed to like us (and our fags) but hated the Yanks. Don't ask me why. That was the end of the patrol for us, we just turned and went back to our positions.

The Commando moved a little further north to a place on the coast called Neustadt and found another concentration camp. It was

[27] Fortunately they did, but they are very small.

in a Marine Barracks and was in such a state that the whole place and everybody in it had to be disinfected. As there were not enough medical people, we had to do it using DDT powder in pumps. All the camp guards and staff were still there and so they were put into one of the huts. It had a barrel as a lavatory and the bunks were all in a terrible state. They complained that it was inhuman to put them into a hut that was filthy! Our bloke just said to them, 'You had all those people in here. You are being treated as you treated them. If you can't hack it for a little bit ... Shut up or I'll set fire to the bloody hut.' And he meant it, although by doing that he would have been lowering himself to the level of those people. Commandos may have had a reputation, but we had a code of discipline and behaviour.

Then it was interrogating prisoners, sorting out ordinary soldiers from SS.

In the bay lay a ship, the *Cap Arcona*, full of dead Russian, Polish and ex-concentration camp prisoners, which had been bound for somewhere when it had been sunk. All around, bodies were afloat or had been washed up on the beach, many with bullet holes in the head. There were mass graves all along the beach.

Shortly after, word came round that the war in Europe was over. I lit a fag, had a cup of tea and went to sleep.

* * *

At Commando HQ my job of mines and demolitions came to light, so then it was daily collection of weapons and explosives and disposal of them in the lake. This got quite boring after a while, but then on one particular day a group of us was taken to a big relay station with four metal pylons and a building full of radio equipment. It had sustained a lot of damage but was repairable. We were ordered to destroy it. We blew down the pylons, cut them into sections, smashed up all the radio kit with sledgehammers and then destroyed the buildings. The reason? It was going to be in the Russian zone.

A few days later I was on sentry duty in front of our headquarters and smartened up like I hadn't been for months, scrubbed, creases in my trousers, shiny boots, beret on dead straight, cap badge gleaming. A car arrived and out got Bungy Young, our former CO, followed by an entourage. He came up the path, so I came to attention two-three, sloped arms two-three, stop two-three, stop away, present arms up two-three, out two-three, down two-three. Stiff as a rod. He looked at me, came across, said, 'Ah, Scott. How are you?' and put his hand out to shake while I was there at the present. I shook his hand and said, 'I'm all right.' Then I thought, 'You don't do that at the present!' He just walked on laughing! We found out afterwards that Bungy had come back to prepare to take us out to the Far East.

A little while later, we were ordered to pack, and left for Bremerhaven where we got on a Landing Ship Tank. The Provost Sergeant announced that any enemy weapons must be handed in, so as the Matelots on board all wanted souvenirs, we traded with Jack Tar. Pistols, knives, cameras and things, for tinned food, tobacco, anything that was rationed in the UK. It was a nice calm journey and the LST brought us back to Tilbury.

Chapter 12

Joining the Military Police and Leaving the Army

After disembarking, a train took us to a camp at the Goodwood racecourse. A couple of days were spent getting sorted out and cleaned up and then followed two weeks leave. Upon our return, it was back to Worthing to recuperate and re-train in readiness for the Far East. Reinforcements arrived via members of 2 and 9 Commandos.

At this stage there was a little bit of trouble because they wanted to change our weapons for American ones. The Garande rifle, a semi-automatic with an eight round magazine was OK. 1 and 6 Commandos had used them in North Africa, but critically, our Bren guns were to be changed for BARs. We said, 'No. The one thing we keep are the Brens.' The BAR was useless. Every Troop refused. We kept the Brens.

Everyone was issued with 44 pattern webbing, jungle gear, and so we thought, 'Burma'. My name was down for a two-week course at Lewes dealing with Japanese mines and demolitions. The night before going, news arrived that the Americans had dropped an Atomic bomb. 'What the hell is that?' A few days into the course they dropped another bomb. Before starting the next part of the training the officer in charge said, 'Well it's all over. Don't do what's not necessary. Take the 15 cwt Bedford and go into London for the day.' So no Burma trip or Pacific cruise.

The Commando carried on training as usual, but rumours began to circulate about our future. Then news came through that the Army Commandos were to be disbanded. Never mind that every special force, with the exception of the Long Range Desert Group, had come out of the Commandos. 2 Commando were the first Paras and the SAS started with David Stirling of 8 Commando. So that was that.

My mates had never seemed to show fear. I tried not to, but we had all been afraid of something like being maimed, blinded or burned. Better a quick bullet in the head. Morale had always been good. We laughed at anything and everything, taking the rise out of the world in general. It was the end of an era.

* * *

I was sent to the HOC Wrexham and worked on a farm driving a tractor until finally being returned to my own Regiment, the Queen's, at Milton Barracks, Gravesend. Upon arrival, I just walked straight in. There was no guard on the gate and nobody in the Reporting Centre. I thought, 'If a**holes could fly, this place would be an aerodrome!' Suddenly I heard, 'Oi, you!' I kept on walking. 'Oi, you!' Again I ignored it. There was the sound of hob-nailed boots running after me and then I was caught by the arm. I turned around and found myself facing the Provo Sergeant, no medal ribbons, nothing. A typical base-wallah. 'You with the funny hat. When I say stop, you stop.' I said, 'My name's not "Oi" and this is not a funny hat, it's a green beret. Grab my arm like that again and I'll eradicate your nose.' I then walked off. He was totally gobsmacked. No one had ever dared speak to him like that, but there were no repercussions.

For the first few days, everybody ignored me because in effect, I had deserted the regiment by volunteering for the Commandos. However, a little later a truckload of men who had done likewise arrived and I had some 'friends'.

I signed to stay on in the Army and volunteered for the draft going out to Germany to join the 2nd Battalion. I got out there to find that they were being disbanded as well! And so, while in a transit camp at Osnabrück, a recruitment officer in the Military Police gave us a lecture. I took no notice. Who wanted to be a copper? He said, 'Anyone who is interested, please see me afterwards.' He must have smoked a packet of cigarettes waiting. At the end of the day I went down to the Orderly Room to see what the orders were for the next day. On the board was a notice that said, 'The personnel listed below are to be packed at 0900 hours the next morning and will report to the Military Police School at Paderborn, Sennelager'. My name was on it. Straight away I was in the office to complain, but to no avail. Apparently they picked out blokes with good military conduct and I was one of them. My attitude then was, 'Well, if I have got to be a copper, I'll be a copper, and make a good job of it.' Six weeks of training followed, mainly in the classroom on things ranging from Military Law to flags on cars! After a while I realized that it wasn't too bad and the food was good. I passed out number one in the class. They could not fathom me out. Afterwards, amongst others, I began to train Israeli Military Police for the Israeli Army. Eventually I took a group down as far as Brussels before they travelled to Calais and out to Palestine. Their mentality was crude. Everybody had done their bit to liberate the concentration camps but now it was, 'Us against everybody. Get the British out of Palestine.'

I was posted to 247 HQ Provost Company, whose duties were to police the military personnel in Brussels.

The Company Commander was Captain Steadman, DLI. I didn't like him. He was clueless. On one occasion he said to me and a certain Lance Corporal Keary, 'Come with me,' and we went to the north end of the Rue Neauve. He briefed us. 'I shall walk twenty-five paces in front and any soldier who does not salute me, stick him on a 252.' This was the Military Form for a charge. Accordingly, we proceeded south along the road. Of course, soldiers on leave absolutely love to salute officers. They crossed the street, looked in shop windows, did about-turns, anything but the correct thing. We nicked them for 'Failing to pay compliments to an officer when badges of rank were apparent.' Back at the unit this affected their leave, they lost pay, privileges and liberty, all for a tosser of a Rodney. Of course, it left us with the problem of writing more than fifty 252s. Most of them were binned. Personally speaking, any squaddies of the RE, RA and Infantry Regiments were safe from me, unless of course they got a bit stroppy. Mostly I targeted base-wallahs who would flog anything, rations, petrol, blankets, to get money for their bits of crumpet. So if you were RAOC, RASC or some third echelon geezer, tough!

I teamed up with a bloke called Jock Pearson, KOSBs, and very quickly we became half of the riot squad, getting any jobs that were a bit on the rough side, as we didn't sod about! If a soldier was being 'naughty' I didn't go up and say, 'Excuse me old son . . .,' there was only one answer.

Most squaddies didn't like Red Caps until they needed help, especially when being AWOL. Then it was, 'Please, I want to give myself up.' The usual reasons were 'Run out of money' or 'The old woman has left me.' After seeing their COs they would get anything from seven to twenty-eight days punishment.

A few weeks after arrival I was promoted to corporal for helping to thwart a raid on an Army postal lorry. Three yobs bounced the lorry at the Place Rogier traffic lights. I was on a tram, saw the action, but couldn't do a thing until a jeep carrying Polish MPs came alongside. I jumped from the moving tram into the jeep, and we chased and stopped the lorry, catching two of the three thieves. The sergeant in charge and sentry in the cab were also nicked for neglect of duty.

Promotion meant being shunted to the Motorcycle Section, of which I took charge shortly after. The Section was used for escorts, club raids and extra discipline checks throughout the Brussels Garrison. I had six motorcyclists and just sent them out on patrols to anywhere I thought fit. However, they were employed mostly at night for extra duties, this was after a day's work, with no day off afterwards. One of these duties was the catching of black marketeers, mostly Yugoslav soldiers, displaced persons who now worked for the Control Commission Germany, and Poles of the Polish Brigade on leave. British squaddies had no money for the rackets, they spent it all on the beer, birds and fun trails. We would carry out contraband checks at the Gare du Nord when the leave trains were returning to Germany. These people had pockets the length of their greatcoats to stash items and we confiscated alcohol, coffee, tobacco, nylons, all bound for Germany and the black market. Every night a post office sack would be filled with boxes of cigarettes which were recorded and stored at the HQ in Rue de Minimes, eventually to be distributed to the Red Cross and Military Hospitals.

These checks went well, but gradually we began to notice the absence of the Yugoslavs and Poles at the station and guessed that they were boarding the train at Scharbeck, a northern suburb of

Brussels where it stopped to take on water. I suggested a tactic to our Company Commander, who agreed to it. We did our check at the Gare du Nord, let the train go, jumped on the motorbikes, tore off down to Scharbeck, got round the back of the station, left the bikes and waited. As the train pulled in, the Poles came out of the woodwork! I let them get on the train, then walked over, got on and spoke to the train commandant. Being a military object, every such train had an officer and a guard of half a dozen soldiers. Having Captain Steadman's permission I said to him, 'I'm sorry Sir, but I've got to hold the train.' He said, 'You can't do that.' 'Yes I can. I'm holding the train. You don't move until I say so.' In the meantime I had detailed my men to move from the front and rear of the train to meet in the middle. Everything they found was thrown out of the windows. Kitbags full of cigarettes, perfume, alcohol, stockings, coffee, you name it, were found. It stopped them dead. There was no escaping Scotty and his Motorcycle Section!

* * *

Soldiers of all nationalities on leave look for the three sources of strife, booze, food and women. On 20 May 1946 I was off duty with Jock, having a drink outside a café when a jeep shot by carrying Corporal Turnbull and a full crew of MPs. Shortly after, another went by. When a third one approached I flagged it down and asked what was going on. 'There's a riot at the Café Blighty,' a favourite NAAFI Club for Garrison people and men on leave. The 1/5th Camerons, stationed at the barracks next to the Palace de Laeken, were in town for a night out and two of them were in the bar with their ATS girlfriends. They went to get a drink and upon returning to the table found two gunners of 619 Battery Royal Artillery chatting the girls up. There was an exchange of words and the Camerons spoke with their fists. Each called in reinforcements and 247 HQ Provost Company had a number one problem on its hands! We jumped on the jeep and away it went. When we got there the MPs from the first two jeeps were still outside. I asked what was going on. They said, 'We don't know.' 'Well, what are you going to do about it?' 'Don't know.' 'Where's Corporal Turnbull?' 'He went in, up the little flight of stairs and a Jock kicked him in the face and he fell down the stairs.' 'What happened then?' 'The Jocks chased him down the road!' I said, 'Right. Let's sort this out.' I knew the layout of the place well. As you walked in and looked up, there were three levels, each with a veranda all the way around. The rooms off these verandas were bars and restaurants. The centre of the ground floor was 'the pit', a large bar. Rather than just commit my men to a brawl, I split them into sections and gave instructions on where I wanted them to go. In we went. 'Everybody out!' and those that moved were lined up by a crew outside. The fight was taking place in 'the pit' and was still going well. We went up to the top floor. In each corner were fire hoses, so I got four men and said, 'On my signal start hosing them down.' Within minutes they were all swimming! The café was wrecked and flooded. About eighty percent of the Camerons were put under close arrest and 619 Battery confined to barracks. A court of enquiry followed, but we knew nothing of the outcome.

Another memorable night was when I was called down to a café on the Place Rogier. I pulled up in a jeep with two lance corporals to find a large crowd outside looking in. Ordering my men to wait where they were, I walked in. The café was empty apart from a character sitting there on a chair who looked up at me as I came through the door. All around was devastation. Upturned chairs and tables were everywhere, pictures, mirrors and bottles had been smashed behind the counter, and he had pulled the beer pumps out. Great jets were spouting up and the floor was awash with beer and broken glass. I looked at this figure, weighing him up. He must be about five feet ten inches tall, a decent sized bloke. He got up and I then saw that he was Polish. 'Bloody hell.' He started hurling abuse in English, 'F****** MPs, you b*******.' I just stood there. Then he decided to come for me. I stepped aside, put my right foot out, he went over it and as he fell I whacked him around the back of the head. 'Drag him out!'

* * *

While on a jeep coming down the Rue Provencale, I saw this three-ton truck of ours, a little knot of Jocks and one of my little lance-corporals standing beside them. He was telling a Jock sergeant to get on the lorry. But he was refusing, saying, 'I'm a sergeant, you're only a lance-corporal.' My man said, 'I'm a Military Policeman.

You'll do as I tell you.' 'No.' As this sergeant wouldn't move, neither would the rest of them. I got hold of a rubber truncheon and went over to him. 'I'm a sergeant, you're a sergeant. Get on the truck.' 'No. I wouldn't get in for him and I won't get in for you.' 'Get in that wagon.' 'No.' 'Sergeant, third time, get in that wagon.' 'No.' BANG, I hit him straight across the collar bone. I said, 'Pick him up and chuck him on. The rest of you, get on that wagon.' On they got. Afterwards I said to the lance-corporal, 'You could have told him all night to get on there and in the end he would have walked away. When you say something, you must back it up.'

With booze and food the problems can be temporary, but VD could be permanent. It called for controls all the time. Consequently the Services provided prevention. Condoms were issued when a unit knew that its men would be going into a place such as Brussels. If a person was somewhat over-zealous and ran out, free condoms were then available from Prophylactic Centres. If it was too late, he would have to put his name in a book, the date, time and place of the incident and then get a clean out! We would then investigate using this information. Red light districts were out of bounds and raids were laid on to clear these localities of squaddies. The main brothel areas were around the Rue Provincial, Rue Zerezo, by the Gare du Nord, the big names being The Black Cat and The Pelican. One night my house of pleasure was The Black Cat in the Rue Zerezo. I made my way there with one jeep and two lance-corporals. We were duly clearing said Black Cat knocking shop of all Service personnel, checking their identities and warning them, when I saw some white gaiters and brown boots under the curtain at the farthest end of the café. I said, 'When I say all out, it means ALL out!' I pulled back the curtain and lo and behold my own RSM was sitting there! I must be the only bloke in the Army to have exited his own RSM from a brothel! This of course made it dodgy for me, but duty was duty. Next please!

Being a Military Policeman had its good times. There was an incident one evening when Jock Pearson and myself decided to patrol around the back of some of the vice dens at the rear of The Pelican. We came upon two thugs beating up an English sergeant, so we crept up and Jock took one, myself the other. A size nine boot in the wedding tackle and two sharp rights to the chin and it was all over. They had spotted the sergeant, who had just arrived on leave,

135

in the bar with loads of lolly and so decided to separate them. We nicked the sergeant for being out of bounds and sent him on his way, not too badly hurt, but wiser.

Most people recognized that all soldiers had jobs to do and that Military Policemen are primarily soldiers, trained to handle most awkward situations that arise. Many incidents go unsung, such as one night at the top of the Boulevard Adolph Max, when we found a Grenadier Guardsman with no cap, no belt, in what could be called shit order and feeling very sorry for himself. A colleague, Lance Corporal Jim Humphries, had served in the Grenadiers before joining the Military Police and so we got this Guardsman into the jeep and took him back to HQ. Jim had a spare Grenadier cap badge, I had a spare cap and we found a belt. He had a shit, shave and shampoo while we blancoed the belt, polished the brass and cap badge, pressed his battle dress and gave him some grub and a cup of tea. He was given a good talking to, told him to keep his nose clean, wished good luck and returned to where we had found him. One very surprised Guardsman.

Similarly, I helped a soldier from the 1/5th Cameron Highlanders outside the Blighty Club. He was very sick, so I took him back to the barracks at Laeken for treatment. A couple of days later I was alone in a jeep, visiting NCO duties, checking on the various patrols that were out. Quite a crowd had gathered in the Place Rogier so I stood up and saw two Polish soldiers fighting. I slowly drove through the throng and got off the jeep to stop the fight. The result was they both turned on me. This was a bit iffy. One went to give me a right hander, so I parried and gave him a hard right, straight in the mouth. Then out of the corner of my eye I saw number two coming at me, but from the punch of my elbow, he shot straight back with a smashed nose. I couldn't have hit the first Pole hard enough because he then jumped on my back, his head over my left shoulder. Lovely black curly hair was duly seized and pulled, followed by a sharp turn of the hips, an arched back, and crash, he is on his back on the paving stones, his second time down. Just as the other one started again, I spotted a soldier amongst the crowd holding up a Regimental Policeman's badge, a tartan armband with RP on it. This was a signal, 'Do you need any help?' It was my Cameron Highlander. 'Come on in,' said I, and between us we oust the two of them. Jock got a lift back to barracks and they went into the Guardroom and eventually into the arms of the Polish Military Police. They were to put it lightly, most upset!

On another occasion, Lance Corporal Edwards and myself were on the motorcycles following the Rue Provincial up to the canal. There was a taxi in front of me, so I waited a moment until there was a clear road, signalled my intention to overtake and as I passed alongside, the taxi swerved left and would have taken me out, but I accelerated and just got past. However, I had too much speed and ran out of road, directly towards a hoarding built around the cellars of bombed buildings. I braked hard, both front and rear. The bike stopped but I carried on and met the hoardings with my face. Luckily the Military Police insisted that helmets be worn. Lance Corporal Edwards decided to look after me instead of chasing the cab, so we lost the culprit. I finished up in hospital with a smashed cheekbone and Edwards got a bollocking from me!

Acting on information received, a night raid was planned for the Metropole Hotel, Place Broukere. Outside were local gendarmes, Snowballs (US police) and Canadian Provost Corps. Dressed as a squaddie, I went inside and sat at a table with half a dozen Guardsmen. At the appointed hour, in walked our CO, Mr Steadman, with his little leather-bound stick. There was a small band on the stage playing away and he walked up and tapped on the microphone with it. 'Ladies and gentlemen, this is a Police raid. If you all stay where you are, remain seated and get your ID cards out, my men will pass among you.' These Guardsmen went barmy! 'Bloody MPs, they spoil everything!' I stood up and said, 'Sergeant Scott, 247 Company. Can I see your ID passes?' You should have seen their faces, especially after such a tirade! I said, 'Nothing to worry about lads.' Meanwhile two Snowballs looking through the window noticed a bloke open his briefcase and in it was a 9 mm Browning. The Yanks very calmly walked in as if they were customers and one grabbed him while the other took the briefcase. He turned out to be a Zionist terrorist trying to buy guns.

From the Provost Company I was moved to Antwerp, a different Section, but the same work. A nice quiet place, Antwerp, with all those sailors, Canadians, Poles and Yanks. It was a powder keg. We had our work well and truly mapped out, minimum patrols during the day, maximum foot and mobile patrols at night. The times of strife were from 2330 hours until dawn, all over the usual reasons, booze and birds. There was always the same excuse, 'It wasn't me Sarge, he started it!'

After a few weeks of this it was back to Brussels and then on an advance party to Rhine Army Headquarters, Bad Oeyenhausen to prepare billets. We had a 'good drink' in the Mess the night before going. The morning after, I woke up and my God, what a hangover. I walked out in front of the garage above which were some of the billets, and several of the lads were just unloading their gear. A heavy kitbag landed on the ground right in front of me. They had thrown it straight out the bloody window. The vehicles were loaded and I got in the first jeep because I was leading. 'Off we go.' The driver said, 'Where are we going?' 'Germany of course!' 'Which way do we go?' 'Towards Louvain!' We went around Brussels on the ring road about four times. He said, 'Well you're not telling me where to go!' I was just out of it.

We eventually arrived in Bad Oyenhausen and the first thing to be done was organize the bedding. This had to be withdrawn from the bedding store, taken down to Company lines and dumped in the house, where they could sort it out themselves on arrival. For this, a three-ton truck was needed but the RASC driver had gone AWOL. Military Police sergeants were not allowed to drive vehicles above a certain weight, i.e. no three-tonners, but I thought, 'Balls to that, I'll drive the thing.' I went down to the bedding store and was coming back nice and steadily, only to get stopped by the Military Police, to be precise, 101 Company CMP, the Provo Company in the town. There would have been no problem if I had taken my jacket off. I let him say what he had to say and said, 'Look. I'm 247 Company and we're moving up here next week. I'm in charge of the advance party. I find myself in the brown stuff. I've got no driver. What would you have done in my place? If you're going to start harassing us, we're going to start getting on your tits! Our Company's senior to your Company and you'll be in the crap!' 'Yeah, I see your point,' he said. That was that and I drove off.

However, it was not our last encounter with them. A few days later Eddie Edwards came in and asked what we were going to do that night, so I said, 'We'll go down the NAAFI.' Now you just did not drink with your men in the NAAFI, but my Section were my mates. I knew they were all right. I wore a jacket to cover my stripes. We pushed two tables together and I said, 'You know the drill. All go to the bar and get a round of drinks.' The two tables were one mass of pint glasses. 'Right. Start outside and drink towards the middle!' We were all sitting there laughing and joking and in came a patrol from 101, checking identity cards. A sergeant said, 'Evening lads. Let's see your papers.' I said, 'Oh for Christ's sake, Sarge, we're moving up here next week, 247 Provo Company.' He said, 'Yeah, I've heard about you lot.' I said, 'If you're going to start on us, you're going to start a war.' In the end he said, 'I see your point. Have a good time lads,' and away he went. If he had stuck to his guns as he should have done, I would have been in trouble.

The winter of 1946/47 was, to put it mildly, pretty stiff. We had to cease motorcycle patrols and use jeeps with chains on the wheels. The town itself was left to 101 Provost Company while we blitzed the red light districts and black market in outlying towns like Düsseldorf, Krefeld, Münster and Bielefeld. It was surprising what we dug up. There were deserters and in particular, plenty of weapons.

In late January 1947, I was sent to Hamburg to take over 16 Detachment CMP, the section dealing with the war crimes trials. My orders were to get a grip on them because they felt sorry for themselves and were slacking. When I arrived, they were living on the top floor of an old barracks outside town. It had no windows, no fires, no hot water and minimum bedding. The Adjutant of the barracks belonged to the Household Division, Coldstreams, so I asked for an interview. 'What can I do for you?' said this 'Wodney'. 'You have asked, so here goes. Decent quarters, heating, winter-scale bedding, i.e. blankets, decent ablutions and cleaning facilities. You want smart MPs. OK, help us attain that standard. My Deputy Provost Marshal at Rhine Army HQ won't be happy if I report this state of affairs.' This 'Wodney' was a fair bloke and came and had a look. He said, 'God, I knew not of this state,' and got things moving in the right direction. So all the monkeys were happy, that is until I started a nightly two-hour switch-on for all Motor Transport. It was absolutely freezing, so the vehicles had to be warmed up in this fashion until the weather abated.

The actual job was to guard and escort the war trial prisoners from Altona Prison to Court Numbers 1 and 3, and guard them all bloody day. We had to feed them as well. They were from Ravens-bruck and Banterweg Camps, the latter being an Arbeitskommando, an off-shoot of the Neuengamme Camp near Bremerhaven. These had been for people deemed well enough to work. Then they were just worked to death.

The names of those from Ravensbruck, Court 1, were Gottfried Drossen, R.F.G. Guenther, Ernst Hoffman, Hans Horstmann, G.A. Jepson, H.W. Guerig and Otto Theummel. Those from Banterweg, Court 3, were Carl Moller, Anton Nicolaison and Claus Schumacher, all SS Camp staff or Kapo, prisoners used as guards. They were a really sad bunch. Why we wasted money on them is a mystery. A .303-inch or 9 mm bullet would have been quicker.

In April '45 I had seen the effects of what they had done at Belsen and again later at Neustadt, so I knew about what was being said. There were witnesses from every country in Europe and they were all saying the same thing and pointing at the same people.

One bloke recalled an incident he had witnessed in Banterweg and subsequently, the whole court was taken to the camp. He didn't know why, but for some reason one of the prisoners was being punished. He saw him taken outside and crucified on the fire bucket hooks. When the victim lost consciousness he was doused with water, revived and the torture resumed. Each time he passed out, there were more buckets of water. Being winter, in the end the man was hanging there, resembling a block of ice, dead. The witness was asked if any of those present were the perpetrators of the atrocity. The man answered 'Yes' and pointed at Drossen and Hoffman. That was just one incident.

The prisoners were going all over the place to be tried. Once they had been found guilty and condemned to death, they should have been strung up, but no, these people were going from one place to another to be condemned again and again. In the end the authorities would just say, 'He's been punished enough, let him go!' This happened to a lot of them.

One prisoner was taken sick and I was told, 'Sergeant, get transport and take this man back to the prison hospital.' Hamburg is a nasty place to be at that time of year and it was freezing brass monkeys outside. I went out into the road and stopped the first vehicle that came along, a British Bedford three-tonner with an Army Service Corps driver who said, 'I haven't done anything!' 'It's all right. I want you for a job.' 'I've got a job, I'm going ...' 'Sit there. Wait.' The bloke was brought out on a stretcher. All he had around

140

him was one blanket, as good as nothing. I said to the driver, 'Get your tailboard down.' In the back of the lorry he had been moving coal about but it was not too bad, so I said to the stretcher-bearers, 'Bung him on!' The tailboard was shut and I said to the driver, 'Altona, and don't stop, all the way.' We got to the prison and I went in to the courtyard, which was a sheet of ice. Entering the Guardroom I said, 'I've got one sick prisoner outside, to be taken to the hospital.' Two orderlies carried the stretcher across the courtyard, slipping and sliding, and put him down in the corridor outside the Guardroom. I had a look at him and he was still alive, so they signed for him. One live body, one signature, that's all I wanted. Then I went back to the lorry, 'Take me back to the court.' The driver moaned like hell about getting into trouble, but I assured him he wouldn't. We got back and I gave him a chit to say what had happened and went back into court. Half an hour later we got a phone call from the hospital saying that the bloke had been certified dead. Well, as far as I was concerned at least one got his comeuppance.

Hearing stories of atrocities day after day had begun to work on me. During the evenings, after duty I would go down to the Victory Club in Hamburg, have something to eat and sit in a quiet room listening to anything classical, Mozart, Rachmaninov and found it calming, therapeutic. I even went to the opera on one occasion! I also realized that I was smoking, getting through packets of fags like nothing. And I was twitching. I thought, 'Why is this happening now when there is no 'crash, bang, wallop' going on?'

When the court finished I returned to Bad Oeyenhausen, back with the Motorcycle Section. This time I was training motorcyclists and doing normal duties. Then in late April 1947 I went back to the School of the Corps of Military Police at Paderborn, for a trooping ceremony to change the title to Corps of Royal Military Police. This meant ten days of bullshit. Tons of Blanco, Kiwi, Brasso, spit and dusters by the square mile and drill from the screaming guards, drill pigs who enjoyed themselves. Then the day dawned. I was a marker with a guidon (flag) and stood to attention for five hours. Roll on NAAFI break! I was really cheesed off. It was a good job, I would not run the Military Police down, they are there for a purpose, but all this mucking about was not my idea of soldiering. I kept handing requests to our Orderly Room Sergeant, Clewes, for a transfer to the

Paras, but nothing happened. I was forever asking him, 'Any news about it?' 'No.'

By this time I was feeling a little better. My good mate, Jim Humphreys, the Grenadier Guardsman, had helped me quite a lot. I wasn't drinking but still smoked too much. However, there were a couple of incidents. At Christmas we did 101 Company's duties at Detmold. Travelling back, I knew the road and that the bridge over the autobahn was down, but as I neared where it should have been, it was obvious that someone had taken the diversion signs, the lamps, everything off the road. It was a sheer drop and if any vehicle had come down the road it would have gone straight over, but luckily my jeep was the first to come along. I put the vehicle on the grass verge in the middle (there were no crash barriers) and quietly walked forward along the grass. At the last minute the perpetrator must have twigged that I was onto him. He jumped up from the bank and began to run towards my jeep. I drew my .38 Enfield and knelt down so that I could see him against the skyline, but only his head was visible, bobbing up and down. My first two rounds missed, but down he went on the third. He had been hit in the leg so I picked him up, slung him in the back of the jeep and handcuffed him to both side rails. He was bleeding but I didn't have any first-aid kit. I went back, dragged the diversion board across the road, re-made the lamps out of the wreckage and put them in position, then returned to the jeep and drove away. All the way back to Bad Oyenhausen he would not stop going on about being wounded. 'Shut up!' I went into the Orderly Room and reported. The Orderly Officer turned up and was informed about what had happened. 'Where is this man now?' 'He's outside in the jeep, Sir.' 'Has he had medical treatment?' 'Not yet.' And so it was 'Oh my God . . .' and all that. Anyway, a doctor was found and the German went to hospital. I looked in the back of the jeep and thought 'Bloody hell. I've got to clear that lot up now.' Subsequently, there was a Court of Enquiry. I explained what had happened and received stupid questions in return. 'Why did you think this course of action was necessary?' 'He had just carried out an act of sabotage and could have caused some of our blokes to be killed. So I shot him. We were shooting these people six months ago and getting medals for it!' They called me callous, brutal, everything under the sun, but couldn't do anything because I was doing my duty. However, they did charge me fourpence ha'penny for three rounds of .38 ammunition! It was in red in my pay book!

The second incident occurred at Bad Oyenhausen Camp. The Officer's Quarters backed onto the railway line going into Bad Oyenhausen Station, and across the line was a shanty town. One evening I was sitting, chatting to Humphreys while cleaning our kit for the next day. A telephone message came through saying that intruders had been seen in the area of the Officer's Quarters. In shirt sleeves and plimsoles, Humphreys and I proceeded to this house, where the German maid told us that someone was in the garden. With only one window on that side, guessing that he would use it, I put Humphreys in the corner by the window and told him not to move, while I sat opposite on the floor by a cabinet and waited. Eventually, after what seemed a long time, a hand appeared followed by a head and shoulders, then a body. My pistol was ready and cocked. 'Come on in mate and I'll blow you straight out again,' but somehow he twigged and began to run. I went straight out the window, followed by Humphreys. The fugitive plunged down the bank, across several sets of tracks and into the shanty town. I fired six rounds at him, but without luck. He was moving too fast in the dark. I must have scared the life out of him though! Of course, six rounds of ammo, ninepence! But this time I didn't pay as I had some spares. After this they said I was trigger-happy. Maybe I was.

Subsequently I handed in another transfer request to Sergeant Clewes, but he said, 'Look Scotty, don't bother. The old man has told me to just throw them straight in the bin. He doesn't want to know.' Well I said, 'That's all wrong,' and went back to my bunk to think about what I could do. Then I remembered that after signing on, you got a short amount of time to confirm the fact. How many days option had I got? Had I passed the date? I checked and found that there were two days left. I went straight back over to the office. 'Sarn't Clewes, I want out.' 'What?' 'I want out. Get my demob papers ready. I've got two days, then finished.' They couldn't believe it. 'You demobbed? Not possible.' My idea was that I would get home, complete the fifty-two days demob leave, during which you were transferred to the Reserve, and then enlist in the Paras. In two days it was done and I was away.

From the Hook of Holland, I was shipped across to Harwich and then by train to the Military Demobilisation Centre at York. We chose our civilian clothing pretty quickly. They had everything, shoes, socks, suits (or jackets and trousers), shirts, ties, hats and raincoats (you could keep your Army greatcoat for a pound). Some people changed into civvies straight away, others used the cardboard boxes provided. After we finished the check out, there were spivs at the gate, ready to buy your demob suits or clothing! It was back to York Station, and I just had time for a drink before the train to London and home. It was 9 August 1947.

So it was out into the big wide world of Civvy Street with its bitchiness, ration cards, black market dealing, mostly overlooked by the authorities, restrictions of all kinds, and the difficulty of finding employment. People were whingeing and telling you to forget the war, 'We suffered as well.' All the hardship stories from people who earned good money, slept most nights in their own beds and enjoyed a life in ninety percent safety. Even relations told me of their horrific experiences during the V1 and V2 bombs: 'It was in the Old Kent Road area over south London.' 'But you were in Tottenham!' 'Yes, but we never knew where the next one was going to land.' Sailors on the North Atlantic convoys and the PQs to Russia were ridiculed and we were told, 'Don't talk about D-Day, North Africa, Italy or Burma, we read about it in the newspapers. A piece of cake!' People would ask me about the fighting, 'Didn't you feel anything?' My answer to that was half the time you didn't see the enemy. It was very rare that you saw the bloke you were shooting at. We were trained to hit that target silhouette, just aim and squeeze the trigger. If he went down, he went down. After the first couple, you were just using a weapon. That was that. You didn't have time to wonder whether he was married or had kids. If you started thinking like that, you were lost. If you hesitated to pull the trigger, the other bloke would not, and he wasn't worrying about whether you were married with kids.

After the cliquey camaraderie of Army units, Civvy Street proved to be a lonely time. One suddenly felt isolated. The family wanted most things (some unobtainable) straight away. Then the usual remarks: 'Things are getting worse since you came home. When are you going to get a job?' Forget about the fifty-two days leave, the hoped for, expected joy, all the time dreaming of Civvy Street and some comfort and relaxation. Where was this country fit for heroes? After about six months of Civvy Street a lot of blokes re-enlisted.

I hung around for a while, then went to the Army Recruiting Office behind the British Museum. I walked in and the recruiting sergeant said, 'Hello son. Want to join the Army?' I said, 'Cut it out. I'm on demob leave, but looking at the feasibility of re-enlisting.' He lost interest! 'What mob were you with?' 'Military Police.' 'Rank?' 'Sergeant.' 'Go upstairs and see the Major.' I went up and saw him and he said, 'Oh yes, we'll get you back in. Same mob, same rank . . .' I said, 'I do NOT want that. I want to go to the Parachute Regiment.' 'I can't promise that.' I said, 'Look, forget the rank, let me go to the Parachute Regiment as a private.' 'Wait a minute,' and he went out of the room, came back and said, 'It can be arranged, sign this paper.' I said, 'No, I don't sign anything until I'm a committed man.' He came out with all the old waffle about the Paras being in Palestine, but I wasn't worried about that, I would go out there. He said, 'You know you'll have to do the training.' I said, 'Look mate, I've been through it, I know what it's all about, just look at my record.' He said, 'How long did you serve in the Military Police?' 'Not long. Before that I was with 3 Commando.' 'Ah, now I can understand why you want to get in the Paras.' But with all of this talk, he still could not say that he would do the necessary things to get me into the Paras, so I walked out. I would not don the khaki again for another twenty-three years.

Afterword

It was difficult after the war. With people's resulting attitude, ex-soldiers began looking forward to reunions, if only to meet blokes of the same ilk, talk of the good (if any) times and remember those who did not make it home.

In 1970 I joined the Territorial Army Volunteer Reserve and subsequently trained cadets for twenty-four years as a CSMI, followed by nine as a civilian instructor in the Army Cadet Force.

Some fool said young and old cannot mix. Well we do in the Commando Veterans Association. If a man has done the Commando Course, suffered and passed, has merited the Green Beret, been fired upon by Germans, Italians, Japanese, French, Greeks (and Yanks), he is a veteran. No one can take that away from him, and we welcome him into the CVA.

The yearly/monthly reunions remain the best thing in Civvy Street. A little while ago I took a group of ten ex-Commandos shooting. They all made maximums. Eight rounds, eight hits, five rounds, five hits at moving targets. Not bad for old boys of around eighty!

I have never retired. Demobbed, yes, but I have lived like a soldier, as a civilian. Once a soldier, always a soldier.

Appendix

Verdicts on the weapons I used and fired between 1940 and 1947:

Boyes .55in Anti-Tank Rifle – OK for 1935, but heavy. Post 1941, found to be useless.

Boyes L/W Flamethrower – Gruesome six bursts of flame, thirty yards range, suicide weapon.

Bren – Very good Section weapon. Could perform fixed line fire and anti-aircraft.

9 mm Browning – Used by the Canadian Paras. Handle a bit thick but a good weapon.

Carbine (USA) – A light weapon for Rodneys.

Colt 45 – Uncomplicated, good stopping power.

Garande – Heavy, eight-round magazine. Big flash but used by 1 and 6 Commandos and issued to 3 Commando in 1945 prior to the prospective move to the Far East.

Hotchkiss MG (French) – We had a few with no attachments like bipods or tripods.

KAR 98 – German Mauser, Mauser bolt, five-round magazine. No rapid rate of fire.

MG34 and 42 – Good weapons, light role or fixed lines.

2-inch Mortar – Good for HE at 450+ yards. Illuminating and smoke, high and low angle. A useful platoon weapon.

3-inch Mortar – Ten pound bomb. A good crew's rapid rate of fire would be eighteen to twenty-two bombs in the air.

51 mm Mortar – Cumbersome.

81 mm Mortar – Very good.

MP40 Schmeisser SMG – Excellent.

Nagent Carbine (Russian) – Fired once. Shocking.

PIAT – Another suicide weapon.

.38 Smith & Wesson – A John Wayne weapon! Had this in the desert. Similar to the Colt 38 Police special. Wasn't bad, but would not have liked to use it against the Germans.

SMLI No. 1 Mk 3 – The best bolt action rifle. The Lee bolt and ten round magazine made a very good manual rifle. Line Regiments were trained to fire fifteen rounds a minute. Commando soldiers were trained to fire thirty rounds per minute.

Sten – The Mk 5 was the best, copied by Otto Skorzeny.

Thompson sub-machine gun – Easy to clean, good stopping power, made better with the thirty round magazine.

Walther PPK – 7.62 calibre. Lovely little weapon. I'm not surprised James Bond used it! Very smooth and easy to handle.

.38 Webley – Pretty accurate but lacked stopping power.

Index